C000224708

Poolbeg Press a~

mothercar

Offer you a chance to win a €500 mothercare gift voucher

mothercare is your one stop shop for all your nursery needs, so for that wonderful, frustrating, hilarious, serious, exhausting, rewarding process called parenting we're here.

Come in and enjoy spending your voucher at any of our 17 stores nationwide. You'll be sure to find everything you need for all bumps and babies.

For more information about **mothercare** visit www.mothercare.ie

To win this fantastic prize all you have to do is answer this question: What animal jumped over the moon in the famous children's nursery rhyme?

Answer: _____

Name: _____

Contact number: _____

Postal address: _____

Email: _____

Send this page in an envelope to: *Over the Moon* competition, Poolbeg Press, 123 Grange Hill, Baldoyle, Dublin 13.

over the moon

Contributors

Claire Allan
Maeve Binchy
Adam Brophy
Amanda Brunker
Paul Costelloe
Brendan Courtney
Paul Cunningham
Ian Dempsey
Anne Dunlop
Niamh Greene
Emma Hannigan
Lorraine Keane
Sheana Keane

Cathy Kelly
Mary Kennedy
Sonya Lennon
Fiona Looney
Frank McNally
Sean Moncrieff
Sinead Moriarty
Pól Ó Conghaile
Áine O'Connor
Liz O'Donnell
Mary O'Rourke
John Waters

ROYALTIES DONATED TO

OUR LADY'S
CHILDREN'S HOSPITAL,
CRUMLIN

over the moon

How children changed my life

POOLBEG

Published 2009
by Poolbeg Books Ltd
123 Grange Hill, Baldoyle
Dublin 13, Ireland
E-mail: poolbeg@poolbeg.com
www.poolbeg.com

1 3 5 7 9 10 8 6 4 2

A catalogue record for this book is available from the British Library.

ISBN 978-1-84223-375-7

Typeset by Patricia Hope in Sabon 12/16.75
Printed by Litographia Rosés, S.A., Spain

www.poolbeg.com

Acknowledgements

Poolbeg Press would like to thank all contributors to this book for their great generosity in writing about such a personal subject, especially under time pressure and given their busy lives. We are also grateful to Our Lady's Children's Hospital, Crumlin, especially Janet Dunphy and David Doran of the Children's Medical and Research Foundation at the Hospital, for working with us on the book and for all of their help.

Contents

Foreword   xiii

Introduction by Sean Moncrieff   xv

Claire Allan
This Scary Little Thing Called Parenthood 1

Maeve Binchy
Borrowing Children   9

Adam Brophy
Overtime   13

Amanda Brunker
My Guilty Pleasures   23

Paul Costelloe
A Design for Life   31

Brendan Courtney
The Eternal Uncle   39

Paul Cunningham
Wonderwall   43

Contents

Ian Dempsey
Reasons to be Cheerful, 1-2-3   55

Anne Dunlop
My Daughter has Diabetes   67

Niamh Greene
The Super Mammy   77

Emma Hannigan
When Two Planets Collide   85

Lorraine Keane
Baby Bore   99

Sheana Keane
The Secret of Happiness   105

Cathy Kelly
The Love Letter   115

Mary Kennedy
The Growing Years   123

Sonya Lennon
The First Leg   133

Fiona Looney
If . . .   143

Frank McNally
Child-proofing Your Home   149

Sean Moncrieff
Conception   157

Sinead Moriarty
The Imperfect Mother   165

Pól Ó Conghaile
Get on the Bus   173

Áine O'Connor
We've Come a Long Way, Baby   181

Liz O'Donnell
Unconditional Love: A Two-way Street   191

Mary O'Rourke
The Rocky Road to Motherhood   201

John Waters
Free at Last   209

Foreword

Sing not of birthing joys
Mourn not the toddler's knee;
For every child that's born
Makes each of us less free

How soon do we forget
What elders used to know:
That children should be raised
Not left like weeds to grow

The magic of holding your newborn baby as he or she looks at the world for the first time can be overpowering, opening you up to emotions that are almost impossible to imagine in advance. A look, a cry, a touch can stir a deep, overwhelming love.

This beautiful compilation of stories describes the joys of becoming and being a parent: that new kind of responsibility that fills you with joy, excitement and foreboding, which paints a picture that gives genuine meaning to children changing your life and life view forever; which says you have arrived at a destination and life will never be the same again.

Of course, it's normal to wonder how good a parent you are; each person has their own approach. Through these wonderfully personal stories we can bear witness to the many different ways to bring up happy children and marvel that there are as many ways as there are people and that your own approach may not be the only way, or even the best. Heaven forbid, we all sometimes wonder if we are cut out to be parents at all!

At other times, however, there are more serious bumps along the way. Sometimes, the unexpected twists in the journey of parenthood lead to the door of our hospital here in Crumlin. While we don't ever wish to see them here, parents can sometimes become part of our family for as long as they are here.

When they do, we are able to create a supportive environment, thanks to the generosity of people who support our various endeavours, including this book. We want to thank each individual who contributed as a parent to this book and who kindly donated their author royalties to The Children's Medical and Research Foundation. We want to thank those of you who purchased the book for going out and supporting this beautiful publication. Thanks also to those who have supported us in other ways.

Thank you.

David Doran
Chief Executive
Children's Medical and Research Foundation
Our Lady's Children's Hospital, Crumlin

Introduction by
Sean Moncrieff

This is ostensibly a book about parenthood, but mostly it's a book about shock. That one emotion permeates most of the pieces within, from Ian Dempsey's realisation that he didn't know the meaning of the word "busy" until a child arrived, to Liz O'Donnell's feeling of having been "misled by all the books, classes and conversations about childbirth".

As with making babies, the experience of having and raising them is never the same twice, and can never be fully prepared for, partially due to the grinding workload, the radical adjustment of lifestyle, but also because of the profound inner change a child brings. For the adults (and, in Brendan Courtney's and Maeve Binchy's cases, this includes relatives), the world now seems a different place, filled with patterns they had never noticed before.

And this change is all the more astonishing for being humdrum. Every day, in every country on earth, from the swankiest private room in Manhattan to a hut in sub-Saharan Africa, women give birth and understand this miracle.

But parenting is not all about sitting around and being profound. For the most part, it's to do with love and practicality – something Claire Allan demonstrates by writing while pregnant (her second), while Anne Dunlop tells us about the challenges of having a child with diabetes. And in a reminder of how it used to be, Mary O'Rourke writes about having fertility problems when such things were never spoken of.

Pardon the tortured metaphor, but the proud parents of this book are the good people at Poolbeg, who decided to go for a second after the healthy delivery of *With a Little Help from My Friends*, a collection of essays on friendship in aid of the Irish Hospice Foundation. This time, the funds raised will go to aid Our Lady's Children's Hospital, Crumlin – in these economically eviscerated times, a worthy cause if there ever was one.

Just in case you didn't spot it, the title of this book comes from the nursery rhyme *The Cat and the Fiddle*. It also describes the euphoria that many parents at least initially feel on the arrival of a new life. However, *Over the Moon* is also a well-worn cliché spouted by soccer managers; the other being *sick as a parrot*. Hmm. *Sick as a parrot, over the moon*. Probably a confusing title, but that would have been appropriate too.

This Scary Little Thing Called Parenthood

Claire Allan

I write this while heavily pregnant with my second child – the challenge of writing about the joys and blessings of parenthood weighing on my mind much like the weight of my currently huge stomach on my lap.

I have, today alone, been kicked in the thighs by an overactive baby in waiting, been sick (thankfully not in a public place on this occasion) and made noises akin to a cow mooing in a field each time I have had to stand up.

There is no blooming – no Ready-Brek glow of maternal joy and love. There is me – really rather fat, burping 25 times a day and wondering which of the two remaining maternity outfits that still fit will make me look less ridiculous. (My over-the-bump work trousers are winning the battle at the moment after a near-humiliating incident involving my maternity jeans, some slippage and the biggest pair of white cotton knickers known to man.)

Pregnancy is not something I do well, or with any hint of grace or style. There isn't a chance in heaven that at any stage you will ever see me on the front of a magazine, in the nip, clutching my bump *à la* Demi Moore and looking all earth-motherly. There is, perhaps, a very small chance that Gaviscon will ask me to be their official spokesperson as I appear to have consumed so much that I would do well on their board of directors – but that's hardly the glamorous look most people are going for, is it?

I certainly didn't think I would find pregnancy such a challenge. When I was pregnant with my first, five years ago, I assumed I would indeed bloom and develop that Doris Day glow. I imagined long hours of rubbing cocoa butter into my expanding tummy while playing my unborn child a selection of classical music and chattering to him or her about the life we would have together. In fact, the very night I got a positive result on a pregnancy test, I stood at the window of the room which would become the nursery and told our baby just how much he or she was already loved.

I had great plans – to eat healthy, do antenatal yoga and opt for a completely drug-free birth. That changed. Quickly. As soon as the first whiff of morning sickness kicked in I opted for the "eat whatever stays down" approach to pre-natal nutrition, and as for the pregnancy yoga? One session with a very nervous instructor afraid of setting me off into an early labour put paid to that.

We'll not even talk about the drug-free birth – which was, let me just say, never really going to happen anyway. I'm the kind of gal who would opt for an epidural for a stubbed toe.

Still, my son, a gorgeous now five-year-old, was indeed worth it. It did, however, take me some time to realise that – succumbing as I did to postnatal depression after his birth.

While ultimately that experience prompted me to make the bold step of finally writing the novel I always talked about, it wasn't a barrel of laughs at the time. Funny though – it wasn't the horrendous experience I imagined depression to be either. The thing is, it just kind of happened. It became the norm to feel a little out of kilter and I suppose like most new mums I put it down to the baby blues or a serious lack of sleep. Always being one to covet a good 12 hours a night – or more when the chance arose – I did not cope well with the lack of sleep which accompanies a colicky newborn.

So, feeling down was the new feeling normal – it's strange how you don't even really notice it in yourself. Until, that is, you (and by you, I of course mean me) find yourself sobbing into a glass of wine over lunch one day with an old school friend you've not seen in five years. (The poor pet was getting married that weekend and there was me sobbing about something totally incoherent instead of having the happy-go-lucky pre-wedding brunch she had probably anticipated.)

It was only on the road to recovery that I realised just how wrong it had been to feel the way I had. I still functioned remarkably well – tending to all my son's needs like a real pro and putting on a great face to anyone from the outside world looking in. I think I even fooled myself into believing I was happy and a great mammy. It was only when others (including the friend I cried all over) pointed out that they noticed a few strange things about my

3

behaviour (most notably the crying in public at inappropriate times) that I got help in the form of anti-depressants and started to see things a little differently.

Most notably the biggest change was actually feeling that rush of maternal love which I hadn't even truly realised I hadn't felt before. You see, I had loved my son and we had been getting along together quite nicely, but I always thought the talk of that all-encompassing burst of love that parents are supposed to get for their children was greatly over-rated.

It was quite a pleasant shock to the system to experience it, first-hand. Staring at my then seven-month-old son and feeling my heart swell to new levels was amazing – I remember those feelings well and I'm pleased to say that since that time that love has grown and grown to levels I never thought were imaginable. That might sound terribly twee or smug, but it's honest. I know that parenthood brings with it worries and stress, of course, but the love and reward it brings are second to none.

Still, it took me the guts of five years to build up the courage to do it again. And it wasn't – contrary to popular belief – simply because I am such a complete coward when it comes to labour and delivery. Yes, it's very true that during my first labour I did actually ask my darling husband to get out his credit card and pay them – yes, pay them – for a Caesarean or any suitable option to make the pain stop, but that is still not the only reason I dithered for so long over extending my family.

Unlike my mother, who had three of her children in a three-year-period, I am not a glutton for punishment. (Again, if anyone chooses to define this as cowardice, then fair enough – I can't really argue.)

It was more the case, however, that after my rocky start to parenthood first time around, I wanted to savour my son as much as was humanly possible for as long as possible. We formed a bond – a very, very strong mother-and-son bond. There was a definite over-compensation in terms of wanting to spend time with him to make up for the months of fogginess when he was little. And he kept me busy – very busy. With the characteristic inquisitiveness of a toddler, there was little I could do without being asked to explain it, several times and in great detail.

It was hard for me, and my husband, to sit down and think about having to deal with that enthusiasm for life two times over. And it was personally hard for me to put myself in a position where I would be opening myself up to postnatal depression again, except this time I would not only have a newborn to deal with but also a very curious and needy five-year-old. You can't really hide the fits of crying from a five-year-old and there is only so much fobbing off with stories of "something in your eye" or "something sad on the telly" that you can get away with.

There was a lot of soul-searching involved in finally agreeing to take this leap of faith and go into the abyss of pregnancy and what lies beyond again.

And still, we knew we had to do it. They say you know when your family is complete and while my son is the centre of my life, I always felt that there was unfinished business to be attended to. I felt that way even after his birth when I was nursing several intimate stitches, vowing never, ever again and cursing my husband for not handing over his credit card for that C-section at the last minute. Even though I shook my head determinedly and said "Never again" ad nauseum, I kind of knew that some day I would find myself in this position again.

But this time is different (and not just because I'm once again at that completely fat and fed-up stage). I feel "done". I feel as if once I've managed to give birth to this baby (hopefully without needing to beg for an operation), I'll finally be able to be a mammy – proper.

While the thought of being a mother of two scares me even more than the thought of post-partum piles, I was not ready to stop at being just a mother of one. I'm going into this with eyes wide open. I know the risks. I know the pitfalls, and more than that, I have learned – in the last five years – to trust my instinct more than any childcare expert or nanny who writes books talking about what we should expect of our children – when in fact all our children are unique individuals.

I know not to expect miracles and that if I'm not the perfect earth-mother type there is a fair chance my child will turn out just fine anyway. I know that if I don't fall immediately and totally in love with my new baby that it doesn't mean I won't ever have that feeling. In fact I'm mentally preparing myself for getting through the first few months with a new baby in survival mode once again. (Although having not had a decent night's sleep since before my first pregnancy, I'm not expecting the sleep deprivation to be as hard to take this time around.)

I'm prepared for the fact that labour is going to hurt – a lot. I thought I knew that first time around – but, boy, was I wrong. Until you are actually begging someone to perform a medical procedure on you without anaesthetic if needs be to make the pain stop, you will never fully appreciate the joys of labour.

I'm prepared for the post-baby jelly belly. I'm prepared to get six months down the road and wonder what it feels like to carry a proper handbag and not a baby bag stuffed with nappies, bibs, wipes and the one solitary lip gloss still in my possession.

I'm prepared to be seen in public with no make-up and baby sick down my top and not to really care about it.

Because at the end of the day there is no greater adventure in the world than becoming a parent – for the first, second or umpteenth time. Whatever it brings, I know that the good will outweigh the bad and that it shall all be worth it – sleepless nights, morning sickness, postnatal depression and all.

When my baby smiles at me – just like my son smiles at me every day – I shall know it was worth it – entirely.

Claire Allan is a 30-something-year-old journalist and author from Derry in Northern Ireland. She has one son – Joseph – and a baby on the way (due March 2009). She has written two bestselling books, Rainy Days and Tuesdays *and* Feels Like Maybe, *both published by Poolbeg Press.*

Borrowing Children

Maeve Binchy

Of course I wanted children. Bright, gorgeous, loving children. I could almost see them. But it was not to be and 30 years ago things were very different. Fertility drugs were not as developed and adoption was impossible after the age of 40.

So my husband and I went through the sad, disappointed bit and then decided to count the blessings that we already had and "get on with it". There would be no bleating about it being unfair, no wailing to friends about what wonderful parents we would have made. In fact we made such a good job of it that many people believed that we were childless by choice.

We asked our friends and relations to lend us their children and, because we lived in London, children loved to come and stay for their half-term holidays.

I never wanted to steal a baby from a pram, I actually liked them best when they were between 13 and 17, mutinous and resentful, when they hated their parents and their parents hated them. We would invite a child and say that a friend could be brought as well. This was a brilliant idea because they had someone to talk to and grizzle with and share the experiences with.

We would give them a bus pass for the weekend and then I would make my speech. The bad news was that my nerves were in very poor shape and so they had to be home every evening at 6.30 p.m.; that ours was a non-smoking home, but of course if they wanted their God-given right to inhale tobacco they could go out in the rain on the street.

Further bad news was that we would always spend half an hour every evening doing cocktails and scrapbooks. "Doing what?" they asked.

We had a battery-driven cocktail maker and lots of sugary mixes so each evening the children had to invent a non-alcoholic drink. Then they had to fill in a scrapbook of what they had done during the day. This torture was invented to make them see *something* in London; they wanted to spend hours in the clothes markets and, as an ex-teacher, I wanted them to have more to report. So it was often easier for them to go to the Tower of London or watch the changing of the guard. They got used to making cocktails too.

The good news was that if they were 14 we would take them to movies for 16 and over – that made them feel terrific when they went back to school. I used to give them money to buy one supper at the supermarket, and the only rule was there had to be some kind of main course, it couldn't all be dessert.

They never needed to tidy their room and we gave them a sack to clear it the day they left. Our neat spare room was like a pigsty with most of their clothes on the floor.

We never told tales behind their backs, we never laid down the law about their future or their appearance. We were touched over and over by their thoughtfulness and the fact they thought we were easy to get along with.

They grew up as our own children would have grown up. They introduced us to their boyfriends and girlfriends, we have had places of honour at their weddings and have been there for naming ceremonies for their children. Now we have "grandchildren" who seem to think that we are an extra grandfather and grandmother. It's not the same as having our own, but honestly it's very nearly as good. We knew the parents of this young generation when they were confused and complicated teenagers, we have pictures to show how dodgy the hairstyles were and how ludicrous their clothes. We remember their secrets, their hopes and dreams.

I bless those good friends and family who lent us their children, and never minded that we played the roles of ageing *enfants terribles*, allowing them more freedom in some ways than parents ever would, but yet indulging our own anxieties under the cover of having bad nerves.

Our many "children" and "grandchildren" will never really understand what a great role they played in filling a gap that could have been sad and destructive but in the end turned out be so joyful. They remember their visits mainly because we had a pinball machine in our sitting room, let them stay up late, and taught them to eat with chopsticks. I hope that they knew we loved their company. And if they didn't know, they do now.

(Originally published in You *magazine, 28 September 2008. Reproduced with the kind permission of the author.)*

Maeve Binchy's latest novel is Heart and Soul *(Orion Books).*

Overtime

Adam Brophy

"Is it done?" he asks down the phone.

"It's nearly there. We're pulling together the loose ends now," you reply.

"You've been pulling together loose ends for two weeks. This goes to the printer on Monday morning. You make that happen. It makes no difference to me if you don't move from that desk this weekend, as long as it goes first thing on Monday. D'you understand?"

"I gotcha Jim. Don't worry."

Click, line goes dead. You stare at the receiver in your hand. "Prick."

You turn your head back to the screen. You lied, you're nowhere near finished. If the author had given a shit about this project, he might have made a half-decent effort to write a decent book. If the editor felt he was being paid a reasonable rate, he might have bothered his arse sorting out the mess. If your boss, the aforementioned prick, had an ounce of sense he would have briefed the author properly at the outset and the dog's dinner sitting in front of you could have been avoided. You sigh and settle in for a quality weekend proofreading. Again.

The phone rings. What's he want now, you to come and massage his corns?

"Hello?"

"You have to come home. I have pains, I'm going into labour. Now. I'm going into labour now. Now, I'm pretty sure."

"You're wha'? You're pretty sure? Look, it's probably those yokes again – the Branston Pickles, nothing to worry about."

"Ha. Very bleedin' funny. You are a comedian in the eye of the storm. They're called Braxton Hicks and if you ask anyone who's had them they'll tell you they're very painful."

"I know, I know. Look, Jim's all over me about this history textbook and you're not due for another three weeks. Are you sure it's starting?"

"Well, I'm not 100 per cent but my belly is at me and it seems worse than usual."

"Right. Tell you what. Sit tight for a while. If the pain gets any worse or more regular, bell me and I'll be straight home, into the hospital, baby out, bang bang, not a bother. Promise."

"You swear?"

"I pinky promise."

"Okay, I'll call ye in a while."

"Super. If I don't hear from you, might as well tell you now, I'm gonna be late home. Have to get this book boxed off. All right?"

"Yeah, but I hate being stuck here by myself at the moment. You know that. I keep thinking it's going to burst out of me and I'll have to deliver it on my own, all covered in blood and screaming."

"Remember what your one said in the antenatal classes. It'll probably be a slow process and there will more than likely be false alarms. We shouldn't move until we have to, until there's one of the definite signs."

"I can't believe this is the first thing you've ever followed instructions for. It's not fair, you make me look hysterical."

"We'll sit tight until we're sure, until there's one of those definite signs."

"Yeah, like my waters breaking, or a show . . ."

"I don't need the details again, hun."

"You're so squeamish. How are you going to cope?" she laughs.

"I'll be grand. You put your feet up and stick on *Oprah*, I'll talk to you later."

"Bye love."

Click again. Third time this week she'd wanted to go to the hospital. She'd have to give up the curries, the indigestion was causing all sorts of consternation.

Beep. You have mail. From Jim. "Those files go on Monday. I'm leaving now, have a good weekend." Prick.

You get home at eleven that night. She's asleep. You drop the laptop 'til the morning and crawl in beside her. You reach around, it's a long stretch, and caress that bump. You feel better.

"Wake up. Wake up!"

"What? What's going on? What time is it?"

"It's three o'clock. We've gotta go now, my waters have broken."

"Oh, right. Just let me get me . . . y'know . . . stuff . . ."

"MOVE IT!"

Fortunately the traffic out of town on a Saturday morning is light. You both sit, looking straight ahead. You have the good sense not to say a word. Anything you say may not be used in evidence but might lead to you being bludgeoned with a blunt instrument. Let her speak first.

"I didn't know I'd peed myself. When I woke up and the sheets were wet I just presumed the action was starting. I'm embarrassed enough. You don't have to say a word; your job is to be supportive."

You continue to stare straight ahead. Seven hours in a labour ward to be told there is no evidence of the child making an entrance has not improved your anxiety levels. You have already fielded two work-related calls and are facing into a bout of Industrial Revolution textbook shenanigans suffering from sleep deprivation.

In a fit of pique you had informed the midwife of your precarious work situation. She looked baffled. "I think you have more important things to worry about," she had said. Shows how much she knows. Deliver a few babies, think they run the world.

Beepbeep. Text from Mick: "Will you make one o'clock? Macker has that new dodgy box in the boozer. All Premiership matches with Norwegian commentary."

Not likely. Have sheets to change.

She gets into the dry bed and harrumphs. She can't move. Walking is a chore. All her favourite foods give her heartburn. Her feet are swollen, her waist is chafed and her nipples are murder. It's your fault. You'd like to stick around and rub her feet, seriously, you would, but you have to work.

This does not go down well.

"Tell that prick to sling his hook, he could take care of this himself."

"I know, but I have to be careful, we can't afford for me to lose this job."

She grunts in disgust and wraps the covers round her trying to burrow deep into an imagined spot of comfort. There is no comfort, only discomfort. You pick up the laptop and sneak into the spare room.

Eleven o'clock. You come to with your forehead moulded into the keyboard, a line of spittle coating the "ASDF" line. You creep back up on the bump, savouring the warmth, the movement inside. She sighs and moves into you. The lines on her forehead stay there, worried even in her sleep.

When you wake you know it's early by the tone of the light. She's gone, a deep indent marking her previous existence. In the bathroom she basks in a full tub, a facecloth sat over her eyes, rivulets streaming down her cheeks.

"How long you been here?"

It's not water, it's tears.

"Um, maybe four or five. Dunno. Tired. Sore. Sad."

"Don't be sad. We're nearly there."

"Are *we*?"

"I'm doing my best."

"Yeah."

Back to the laptop. It's easier when she's mad.

You work all day Sunday. You're confident if you get in early the next morning you can have everything shipped by midday. Slip the noose for a week or two, maybe throw the CV around. Leave that miserable, slave-driving, sweatshop-running bastard behind and have a chance to get to grips with this fathering lark. You owe her and the kid that. You missed the pregnancy, working twelve hour days and weekends, and there's no sign of a let up.

You saw the glint in his eye when you told him the news. You, all buoyed with the fact that your mickey worked, that you were all man, a baby-maker. Well done you. You saw the glint, the glint that said: "Sweet. You're mine now. You can't walk away."

And he's right. He's been turning the screw for six months. Everything he's demanded, you've supplied. He golfs, you work. He yachts, you work. He barks, you bite.

The tiredness eats you. She has slipped away. This whole process, it's gone on without you. Gaining weight, getting sick, cravings, desires. You caught the highlights at the edges of the days, but her friends and her mother lived it. Now, it's already her and the baby while you struggle on the outside. The baby, the engine inside, driving all this. Her big belly. Her baby. You put your hand on it at night while she sleeps. It moves sometimes, balling a fist at you, wondering who you are. What right has your hand to be there? Creeping in for a coy hello, are you somebody?

But you will work this out. You want in, to be involved, you just don't know what with yet. It's in there, in that skin beachball, driving her mad, making you fearful. And growing, all the time growing, out and out on to your side of the bed. Laying there as you slip silently in beside her, pushing you to the edge with only a threadbare sheet for cover.

"Wake up. Wake up!"

"You're having a laugh, arentcha?"

"No, seriously, my waters have broken. We have to go."

You half snore and reach a suspicious hand over. It comes back sticky and wet. You move fast.

2.00 a.m.

"I have a definite birth plan. No pain medicine, but my husband has a homeopathic birthing kit and he's going to administer remedies as required." She blurts this out immediately after a contraction, sitting up in the bed breathing *into* the pain just like we did in class. She always was a good little learner. You're rubbing her back and have ice shards in a bowl on the bedside locker. You wave the blue plastic homeopathy kit at the midwife and attempt a smile. As she turns away and releases her forearm from your wife's nethers with an audible plop you realise she is rolling her eyes. The lady in the next room screams a primal roar and you look at the plastic box and wonder.

5.00 a.m.

"Just give me the fucking drugs, you bitch. Right now."

You raise your head from the foetal position adopted as defence in the far corner of the room to see how matron will take this delicate request from the possessed entity spewing vitriol and filth in the centre of the room. Matron looks angelic, pristine bun clipped to pristine head, pristine clipboard clipping stuff against matronly bosom. Pristine in the face of madness. Your wife lies bedraggled on the bed, the room splatterpainted with her bodily fluids as she auditions for the child role in the remake of *The Exorcist*.

"That's fine, my dear. I simply needed to hear you make the request yourself. For administrative purposes you understand." She nods pristinely at a man standing hidden in the shadows of the doorway. He advances with a large needle.

Twenty minutes later your wife is back. She plumps her own pillows and marvels at the contractions being monitored by the machine beside her. "Was that always there?" she asks.

"Yes," you reply, "You tried to eat it an hour ago."

"How silly was I?" she says. "Maybe you should get a quick nap. Nursey says it'll be at least two hours before I can push and we'll need you fresh. I'm going to read my pregnancy book while I wait."

8.00 a.m.

"One last try," says the midwife. "You've been pushing an hour, any longer and the baby might go into distress. We'll have to see about another way of getting her out."

She fixes you at the end of the bed, blearily, and tries to focus. Unbelievably, she's smiling. Another contraction hits and you know she's going to do it. Everything comes to bear. Her lips roll back and the groan comes from deep in the pit.

The midwife screams encouragement. "Yessss, that's it. Here comes the head!"

It emerges like a slick and bloody seal. Your daughter. Your daughter is born.

9.00 a.m.

Monday morning traffic on Holles Street. Horns blare up to where you sit three flights above. If you angle your head you can see the cars backed around Merrion Square. A sense of their anxiety floats upwards and you turn away.

Your daughter sleeps in the crook of your arm, her mother in the Spartan bed beside you. Both gnaw their fists, engaged. The baby mewls and shakes her head. You tentatively reach a finger for under her chin and stroke. Her hand reaches for that finger and holds it. Tight.

The room is silent. The corridor outside falls quiet too, a faint rattle of trolley and teacup. You start to weep even as you smile. The phone rings insistently, flashing "Office" in the dim light.

You look down at your girl and think, "We'll call her . . ."

Adam Brophy is a freelance editor, writer, psychotherapist and father to the two most beautiful girls in Ireland. His column, It's a Dad's Life, *appears in* The Irish Times *every Tuesday and his first book,* The Bad Dad's Survival Guide, *is available now.*

My Guilty Pleasures

Amanda Brunker

Guilt is a newly acquired word for me.

Three years ago I didn't understand the term. That was before I had children. Now I have two boys – sorry, scrap that – I gave birth to two seriously busy little people, Edward (three years) and Setanta (20 months), and life as I know it has changed inexplicably.

Sure, I thought I felt guilt from time-to-time. If I left someone waiting at the pub for twenty minutes on their own. If I forgot to collect my boyfriend's dry-cleaning when I said I would. When I forgot my Nana's birthday – again! These would all make up minor guilt moments in my life, which I'd settle with an 'I'm so sorry' and would soon be forgotten about.

I was known as a party girl, after all. Party girls didn't do guilt. They went to fabulous parties and drank free champagne. I remember first being labelled as an "IT girl" back in 1999 and thinking it was the funniest thing ever.

Why? Because I was from a working-class background from Finglas. The term "IT girl" was normally reserved for daughters of society families, not young wans from Finglas. But did I feel guilty about dragging the title down? No way.

I never once felt guilty when I lied about my age to enter the Miss Ireland competition either. I had falsified my application to say I was 18 instead of 17. Nadine Coyle, eat your heart out! I had no clue I was going to win. I just wanted to be part of it. Of course, there was some stress when the franchise holders threatened to dethrone me. But guilt? No.

So after 31 years storming through life, it came as the oddest thing to me when, after giving birth to my first son, I began to felt guilty about everything. And I mean, everything, literally. I now feel guilty about spending three minutes instead of two in the shower. About sometimes only giving them three of their five-a-day meals. About dressing the boys in too many clothes, though it's mostly too little with our climate. For being too strict / not strict enough. For giving them crisps / not giving them crisps . . .

Every decision I now make is laced with guilt, because as a parent, there's not always a definitive rule. And without the aid of a handbook, who knows the right or the wrong way to do things. Although we try to fake it, parents certainly don't a lot of the time. Though parents of other people's kids will always have the "correct" opinions on how to raise your child, of course. I've spent many a park play-date grinding my teeth, listening to other mummies brag about some guy called "Spock" and how he had their perfect children sleeping through from six weeks.

It has also been a struggle to find common ground with my partner on what is the right way to deal with our babies. While my other half will show no guilt on throwing Ed on the naughty step for a few minutes for stealing (another) toy off his younger brother and making him cry, I understand – sorry, maybe I should reword that – I feel that at 6.30 p.m. Edward is just trying to get his Daddy's attention, through whatever means possible. And if being naughty gets his Daddy's attention, mission accomplished.

But then as a partnership we need to be united when it comes to discipline, so even though I'm worrying about whether he's cold sitting out in the hall, I'm feeling guilty about not having my bully of a three-year-old better trained. Because if I was a better mother, my son wouldn't push his younger brother over, and then Daddy wouldn't get annoyed with him . . . and then I secretly wouldn't get a tiny bit annoyed at Daddy for being so tough on our son . . .

Confused? Yes, confusion is another new term to me. While that might sound ridiculous, me being a blonde and all, confusion is most definitely new. Pre-babies, if I came across something that I didn't understand, I ignored it. Being quite a competitive person, I tended to keep away from certain situations/activities/difficult conversations that confused me. If I didn't think I could do something well, I just wouldn't do it at all. I was never a taking-part kinda gal. Unless I thought I could be the best, or at the very least, one of the best.

But when it comes to being a parent, even the simplest of everyday activities, such as going to the supermarket with your child, can leave you questioning your sanity. One minute your child is sitting happily in your trolley as you go about your shopping. Next minute, he's turned into the

Tasmanian Devil because you handed him the second croissant from the left, instead of the one on the right of the basket. They all look, smell, taste the same, but try reasoning that point with a hysterical two-year-old!

Before my babies came along, yes, I'll admit that I was one of those people who looked at dishevelled women coping badly in public places with screaming kids, saying to myself, "My kids will never be like that . . ."

Bless. The naivety of it.

Of course, I didn't understand that it could be near impossible sometimes to control hyperactive boys in such excitable locations as restaurants; and I now hang my head in shame at all the times I tutted loudly when waste pieces of spaghetti or chicken nuggets came flying over to my very grown-up table.

Yes, I now understand that maybe parents don't want to take their kids to child-friendly eateries like McDonalds *again* on a Sunday afternoon, and that it's okay for parents to sometimes zone-out their screaming child, even though they're probably bugging the hell out of everyone else, because this might be their only break of the day. And occasionally parents need time-out too.

But even just thinking about taking time out brings me right back to guilt again. Because that's another thing I feel guilty about – taking time for myself. Thankfully I've outgrown the stage of not finding time to shower 'til about five minutes before Daddy comes home in the evening.

My youngest, Setanta, must have been about fourteen months old before I finally managed to shower in the morning like a normal person. There was just never any time before. It wasn't until he started to find his feet and could defend himself from attacks from his brother that I braved leaving the blighters to watch TV for a few minutes to tend to my own personal hygiene. This might sound ridiculous to people who don't have children, but just wait; one day you'll understand my moans.

Possibly the biggest thing I feel guilty about is being a working mom. Thankfully, unlike most women, I have the luxury of working from home the majority of the time, so that means I get to be surrounded by the little terrors most of the day. And while, sometimes, I would appreciate my work space to be child-free, especially when I've an important business call to take – for which I always have a sneaky packet of chocolate biscuits stashed somewhere to keep them entertained – I love being surrounded by my babies. Yes, they slow me down. Yes, it's a complete pain when one of them is sick and just wants to cling to me. But when I'm away from them, the guilt eats me up.

I reason that time away from them is healthy, which I believe it is. Obviously not total separation, but if I'm not home one evening out of seven to put them to bed, it's not the end of the world. Or so I tell myself.

Spoiling them is something that also weighs heavily on my mind. All working mothers know this feeling. The urge to splurge on whatever *Thomas the Tank Engine* paraphernalia is going; because there's a hole in our heart (not necessarily in theirs) and we feel the need to fill it with gifts or sweets to make ourselves feel better.

Deep down we all know that all our children want – at least initially – is our time. But when we can't give it to them, or haven't the energy to give it to them, we'll throw anything their way just to shut them up for an extra 40 minutes in the evening, so we can try to enjoy a cuppa and some actual grown-up TV for a change.

Just the other day I filled out one of those celebrity questionnaire thingies for a Sunday newspaper about the state of my finances, when kiddie guilt hit me again. There I was happily replying to this nosey e-mail and making jokes about seriously personal questions such as: "How many credit/laser cards do you own?"

Seven questions down . . . "If you have children, have you made financial provisions for them?" While I could argue the point on many degrees, the honest answer was simply, NO. I haven't opened a post office account for either of my boys. Worse still, I haven't even bothered to find time to marry their father yet. Sorry lads. And that's directed at all three of the men in my life.

Before I slip off to drown myself in a litre of gin, please let me leave you on a positive note about motherhood. Because honestly, despite my grumblings, I couldn't have wished for a greater honour than to become a mum, and feel doubly blessed to have given birth to two beautiful sons.

Yes, there have been times when I felt on the edge of despair, like when both sons were teething; when they wouldn't sleep because they were afraid of the howling wind; or, best of all, when the winter vomiting bug ravaged the lot of us, and I found myself almost begging to die from my own discomfort, and of course the pain of three dramatic men, who always seem to get sicker than you!

But being a mother has enriched my world so much that everyday I feel like a woman in love. You know that crazy, cannot-live-without-someone teenage love? My children give me that. And it keeps growing, and my pride keeps swelling and, like all mothers across the planet, I think my babies are the cleverest, most talented and handsome children ever. When I show people their pictures, and they politely tell me they're "very photogenic", I immediately have to apologise after I blurt out, "I know", and replace it with, "Oh, I mean, thank you."

I know it does sounds like a cliché, but when you stick your face into their cot in the morning, and this little happy face smiles up at you and coos, "Mom-may", you can only melt. There is no other rush of emotion that can compare. They may keep you awake all night – and believe me, they have a natural instinct for when you have a big day ahead, and somehow know just when to have a difficult night – but a single dribbly smile, their big eyes lit up with such heartfelt delight at seeing you, can amazingly make it all worthwhile.

Obviously if you're already a parent you'll understand how so little can mean so much. If not, I can't imagine I've sold the concept of parenting to you at all.

But for me, having children was always going to be part of my life's journey. I always wanted them, and now that I have them, I find it hard to remember life without them. Aside from the guilt, comes love, laughter and immeasurable joy that no money could create.

Sure, I know my offspring will bring me much heartache along this journey of ours, but I do hope it's a long road we'll share together. To Edward and Setanta, thank you. You've made me want to be a better person.

Amanda Brunker has been a columnist with the Sunday World *for nine years. Her debut novel,* Champagne Kisses, *shot to the top of the Irish bestsellers list last year and is due to be released in five countries later in 2009. Her follow-up novel,* Champagne Babes, *is due out in July. Her proudest achievements are her two sons, even though she feels they have started to age her in dog years!*

A Design for Life

Paul Costelloe

I was thirty-five when I got married which at the time I thought was quite old, but by today's standard is quite acceptable. I had been very much a single man with no responsibilities, living the single life, and when I got married and started a family, my priorities changed completely.

I was the youngest of seven, my wife also being one of seven, and so children were part of our lives, but having our own was a whole new experience!

Number one, who was to be the eldest of seven (that number becoming a lucky talisman for the family), was literally a life-changing event. I don't know what we thought we were having – maybe an octopus or an alien – but there was a real baby, a "mini-me", and the beginning of a seemingly endless road of parenthood.

I don't remember ever making the decision that he would fit in with our lives, but this is exactly what happened, and his small carry-cot was a regular feature on chairs and under tables of many Dublin restaurants. We brought him everywhere.

Being breastfed definitely helped, not having to cast around for all the equipment for bottle-feeding being one of the many benefits, and very quickly we had forgotten what our lives were like before we had him. Attending the births of my children (all but one – she was late and I was in Frankfurt . . .) really made me bond with them from the start and cutting the umbilical cord was a rite-of-passage as a new father.

I became very focused on my work and having a growing family made me ambitious for a better quality of life. Having a house with a garden was a priority for us, so the children could play safely, as I had as a child.

As the youngest in the family with older siblings and a brother two years older, who was a "blue-baby", I spent a lot of time on my own in our old rambling garden in Booterstown. My father would give me "jobs" – cutting the grass, clearing up leaves, chopping down overgrown bushes – and I would spend hours playing happily, when every day seemed like summertime. My father was very much a man of his time and I love him intensely, with that heartbreaking clarity where I now realise what he went through to bring up a large family. His big hands and the smell of bulls' eyes and Sweet Afton as he pulled a couple of boiled sweets out of his pocket for me!

We had three children under three, all boys, and regularly stuffed them into our old Silver Cross pram for walks along the seafront at Seapoint. As the family grew, so did our pastimes. Running around after little ones requires plenty of stamina and keeping fit is essential, so the children were regulars at squash and tennis matches and played touch-rugby from early on. Going to Croke Park and Lansdowne Road, running around the track at Leopardstown, and the Christmas swim at the Forty Foot on Christmas morning are family traditions and ones I am sure they will continue with their own children!

One thing I realised early on is that children love continuity and, even though I travel a lot for my work, weekends are times I try to spend with them. Even if it's only a jog together on a Sunday morning or a game of tip in the afternoon, I cannot emphasise the importance of making the time for them. They absolutely love and need it and if given, however small, it will stand to them forever! Doing things together and participating in the local life of the area we live in is very important – getting to know neighbours and they us – so there are more than two pairs of eyes watching out for them.

My memories of school are not the happiest, as I did not excel academically. I had to cry to sit my primary, but I had a great art teacher when I was in junior school and she really encouraged me in drawing and in the use of colour, which I found gave me the confidence to pursue my current career. Coming from a creative mindset, I suppose I was more aware in seeing similar traits in my children. On our yearly trips to Inismore, the largest of the Aran Islands off Galway, my idea of true relaxation is cycling off to whatever part of the island needs exploring with art pads, paint-boxes, etc. It's amazing what children can do with a bit of paper and some paint. They are so much more spontaneous in what they see around them, and from such innocent beginnings a passion can emerge which can be sustained all through life.

Nowadays, there is so much emphasis on "being a good parent" that a lot of the fun and instinctive dealings with our children are lost among the barrage of self-help books, dreadful nanny programmes on television and so-called parenting classes.

My guess is that, to have survived through childhood and young adulthood and then to the moment your newborn is put into your arms, gut instinct has a lot to do with how successful the transition will be, and your belief in your gut instinct will see you through, along with some trusty helpers. There was the time our eldest caught his foot in the spokes of a bicycle and my dear friend, an orthopaedic surgeon, came out of theatre, complete with gown, mask and serious manner, to set his leg. Or there is the choosing of godparents who will take an extra-special interest in your child, outside immediate family, until they are twenty-one! Good friends are invaluable, particularly when you're all going through the same "upheaval".

The old saying, "every man needs a clever accountant, a good doctor, and a forgiving priest", is especially true in our house. In the early days my wife seemed to spend an awful lot of time in our GP surgery. Every sniffle, ache or spot was at least a case of bubonic plague come to visit Monkstown. Put a crowd of children together in an overheated classroom and, guaranteed within minutes, they will all have contracted some disease! All of these life-threatening conditions passed on to leave seven children, who are all six feet tall or more, largely unscathed. I've never known a bunch of children to receive so many innovations, but the one good thing we did was to keep a baby-book for each one with their newborn wrist and ankle bands, photo curl etc. . . . which is very sweet to look at now.

We always had pets at home when I was growing up and, in today's sanitised environment, it is not always an easy choice to make. I was never ill as a child and the view nowadays that all our homes are probably too clean has a ring of truth to it, in the amount of allergies prevalent in today's children. The presence of a loved and loving animal far outweighs the negatives and our youngest child, who is very artistic and shy to boot, found an ever-willing and constant friend in our faithful cat. When he died two years ago, he was truly mourned by all of us, having survived a lifetime of being dragged around as an obliging playmate and a move to London, a city not exactly geared towards animals. No walking without a lead, no pooing on the grass, booking kennels a year in advance; who could be organised enough to have a pet under such conditions?

The telling of and listening to a good old-fashioned story is sometimes lost in our technological age. My mother was a New York schoolteacher and reading was very important. We had all learned to read before we started school, and I hope I've passed this on to mine. They still love a story, usually ghostly, in a dark room with plenty of sound effects. Also, hearing about your experiences as a child, the "bold" things you got up to and the punishments meted out to you and your siblings, are all guaranteed to induce great hilarity in the house.

It all passes so quickly that one day you realise you've only got two school-going children left, as all the rest have moved on to the more independent life of a university student, and the end is almost in sight! Not true. Apparently this is the next stage, after the newborn stage, where your parental skills are stretched in an elastic band of advice, financial aid and an ever-ready shoulder to cry on. It's more difficult now than when I was a young adult; everything is more competitive and it's a harder world to live in at every level. Even a place at nursery school now requires an exam for your three-year-old, and if they don't pile the bricks in a certain way they are not "offered a place". To encourage confidence and self-esteem in our children is what, as parents, we all aim for, and good communication and realistic goals are what it's all about.

The older I get, the more I realise that there is no secret ingredient to raising a family. All you've got to go on are your own experiences as a child, adult, husband, father, friend etc. When I became a new father I was convinced that I would do everything differently to my parents – give more time, not be too tired, too stressed, be understanding always, etc. – but I realise that they went through the experience of being a parent exactly as I have. The only differences are the time in which they did it. The format is still the same: to raise children to be independent, honourable and compassionate members of society, and to reach their potential, whatever that may be.

As Bill Gates says in his *Rules for Life*, "If you mess up, it's not your parents' fault, so don't whine about your mistakes, learn from them." To help your children reach this superlative goal is to see them as individuals with good and bad points, to steer them as best as you can towards the time of their own independence and to be there for them always, no matter what!

You can only do this by your own instincts and the love and support of family, friends and the people you meet every day. In your dealings with your children's lives, teachers, doctors, sports coaches, etc., will all have something to say about your child. They might not all be things you want to hear, but they will go towards the making of the greatest gift you will ever have.

Looking back, I think I was going slightly adrift in my life and getting married and having a family brought me back to the stability of my own upbringing, with all its humanity and ups and downs. We're heading back to a more hands-on approach to life and bringing up children with today's exciting possibilities is a real challenge.

I highly recommend this step into the unknown, and in my next life I'll do it all over again!

Paul Costelloe is one of Ireland's best-known fashion designers.

The Eternal Uncle

Brendan Courtney

This is a funny one for me. Not being a father, nor having any immediate plans to become one, being asked to write a story about how children have touched my life feels a little fraudulent. I have never had to watch my partner scream in agony during childbirth. I've never lived the fear and stress of those first few months as you stumble terrified into parenthood, gripped with the terror that this helpless little person's life is in your hands.

BUT . . . I have watched my sisters do it. In fact, my sister Deb's waters broke in my bedroom because I made her laugh. I have seen it first-hand – albeit on the sidelines, but I have been up close and personal at the birth and subsequent raising of my three beautiful nephews, Robert, Eoghan and William, and our newest addition, my stunning niece, Emily.

So, on reflection, I feel very qualified to speak on behalf of all the aunts and uncles who get to enjoy all the super nice bits of childhood and children and then get to "hand them back", as it were. We get to be the good cop to mum's bad cop; we get to spoil them ridiculously in return for which they adore us. But the resounding breakthrough revealed to me from adoring my siblings' children is all of a sudden understanding why *my* aunts and (some) uncles were and are so touchy-feely and feel so close to you. Nobody ever tells you just how strong your love for your siblings' offspring will be. It's weird how much I loved them the minute I saw them; it's as close as I can imagine love for one's own child must be.

But more than that, children bring a kind of energy and fun to a household that has to be experienced to be understood; they inject a new lease of life into a family and they give adults something to focus on when we don't want to talk to each other.

My brother Daniel was born when I was 16. Up to that point, I was the youngest of three and then, wham bam!, a baby was thrust upon us, changing a teenage-dominated, angry house into a cooing nursery and literally taking my parents back a generation. So, from a very young age, I have had babies all around me.

Alongside these experiences of being around children as I was growing older, I also (a number of years ago) went through a crisis of spirituality – what I think most people can relate to as a feeling of "what's the point of the whole thing" – life, that is! I had become increasingly disillusioned by organised religion (nothing new there!) and as a result began a search for my own spirituality and my own "meaning of life". It was a turbulent yet very interesting journey. As I dipped my toe in various sects, cults and schools of thought, I came to my own conclusions (I won't bore you with the details).

I came to the conclusion that, as members of the human race and the dominant force upon this great planet, procreation and ultimately children are our meaning of life. So I group myself in the very important (even if I do say so myself) collective I call the "facilitators", the people beyond parenthood who help out and try to make the journey into adulthood a fun and pleasant one, protected and safe, but most of all, loved.

Brendan Courtney is the co-presenter, along with Sonya Lennon, of RTÉ's Off the Rails.

Wonderwall

Paul Cunningham

My son, James Daniel, is a two-year-old rascal and a rogue. With chocolate-blond locks, intense blue eyes and a pearly-white grin, he's a little man on a big mission: destruction.

To an extent, I'm complicit in his one-boy war. He can deconstruct a room in one minute flat; just before the dinky cars are hurled around, like the seeds cast in a wide trajectory for the ever-hungry pigeons in our local park, he catches my eye. This is the key moment. It's when James is supposed to encounter a stern fatherly glare to warn him of the terrible consequences if he carries on. Instead, he sees his 40-year-old father failing miserably to hide his admiration. And in that act of paternal acquiescence, chaos is permitted to reign. Crash. Bang. Thump. A peal of laughter, as he turns on his heel and charges off – the left arm moving quickly back-and-forward, an apparent secret boy-propeller which fires him on to his next date with destiny.

The scenario is a universal one. It's what little boys do. But that very normality is something I treasure, as James was not always like all those other wobblers, toddlers and, lately, terrors. He was, in a very real sense, terrifying. That's because James had to be delivered, by emergency section, long before his due date.

The moment it was confirmed to Flor and I that her pregnancy was not progressing as it should is seared in my memory, frame by frame, but it's also a bit of a blur. We were attending Holles Street Hospital for a planned scan. It was a day of the usual small-scale frustrations – getting out of work and hoping the hospital queue wouldn't be too long. This was just another routine check-up. Like most parents, we looked forward to them. They were reassuring. The dimensions of our tiny son, such as the length of his femur, would be measured on the ultra-sound screen by the caring medical staff, using highly accurate digital wonders. Their calculations didn't mean much to us – we were always too busy looking at the screen in awe, still struck by the wonder of new life.

This time it was different. The doctor was making perfect sense, but we registered only a phrase here and there and can't be sure exactly what she said: ". . . significant drop-off in baby's growth . . . unclear cause . . .". I remember glancing at Flor. She looked as I felt – the colour had drained from her face. The doctor seemed to be telling us that our baby could be born with any number of genetic or other chromosomal conditions: Edwards Syndrome, Down's Syndrome. What did this all mean? It was as if an invisible hand had roughly grabbed the back of my collar and constricted the airflow into my lungs. I tried to loosen my tie and felt close to fainting.

As a reporter with RTÉ News, I've worked in many disaster zones and witnessed how horrible things can happen to children. From diseases precipitated by floods in Mozambique, to lost limbs caused by landmines in Lebanon, to the trauma of ethnic cleansing in Bosnia. But it's a truism to say that things only become "real" when they happen to you, or to someone close to you. Otherwise, the human condition leads us to empathise but not to really understand. The harsh reality is that it was possible for me to report on mostly preventable misery during the day – and then enjoy a beer that night. Why? Because it wasn't personal and therefore I could compartmentalise it, and do so quickly.

As it turned out, James was not growing as quickly as he should have been due to a condition Flor had developed, called "pre-eclampsia" or "pre-eclamptic toxaemia" – a problem usually associated with first pregnancies, but not totally unusual with the second. This is a pregnancy-induced hypertension which affects mothers, usually in the later stages of pregnancy. Pre-eclampsia causes slow foetal growth which, if untreated (the VHI website warns), can develop into eclampsia – a serious, life-threatening condition that can result in stroke or death for the mother. Thankfully, the great medical team at Holles Street had accurately identified the problem in time. The aim now was to maintain the pregnancy for as long as was possible but, if high-blood pressure became a problem, an emergency section was going to be required. Around 50 per cent of babies in Holles Street ICU are there because they are twins. Pre-eclampsia is the second most common reason that they're admitted to the unit.

Our consultant, Professor Fionnuala McAuliffe, is one of those people who exudes a calm confidence. She's direct, but considerate. She's fun, but firm. She's an extremely hard-working, conscientious doctor who, we felt, was very clear on what balance had to be struck between doing everything to ensure the pregnancy continued while, all the time, preparing us for the eventuality that this baby would not reach full term (40 weeks).

The pre-eclampsia was diagnosed during week 29. Flor was given drugs to try to speed up our son's lung development and told to take it very easy. The hospital visits were now daily; each successive day that she was not rushed to the delivery ward was a small victory, as his growth and development were pushed a little further down the road. The hope was that we would make it to week 34, as the baby's lungs would by then have developed fully. This is important as, otherwise, the newborn baby boy would require a ventilator, which can complicate matters considerably.

So we waited and hoped nothing would happen. As part of our preparation for the upcoming events, we were taken on our first visit to a place which would soon become a second home – the National Maternity Hospital Neonatal Intensive Care Unit. From experience, the hospital recognised that any parent likely to have a premature baby needed to have the ground prepared. We were about to discover a little about what the future would hold.

Unit 8, as it's known, is located on the top floor of the hospital. You can only gain admission if buzzed in by a member of the medical team. After the obligatory washing of hands, we began to walk along a short corridor to where James would be rushed in a mobile incubator within minutes of birth. To our right, there was a spectacular view of Dublin's Georgian rooftops. Our focus was straight ahead, though, where, when doors opened, we could see incubators nurturing babies wired up to large machines. The vast majority of the nursing staff here come from the Philippines and their gentle, lilting voices would become so familiar to us over the next few weeks. These women run Unit 8 with efficiency and endless good humour, around the clock, attending to squawking babies and bleeping machines – making huge efforts to preserve and nurture tiny fragments of life.

Flor and I were given the tour. Though we tried to listen, our attention was drawn to the size of the babies in these see-through boxes. They were so much smaller than we'd expected. Arms and legs like pencils. Little faces which were perfectly formed, but in miniature. Just when you thought you'd seen the smallest possible human being, another would be spotted. Could our son be that small? And if he was, what were his chances of making it? That's when the penny dropped for me – the very survival of our son was in the balance.

With our short visit over, Flor and I turned to leave and were shown down a corridor festooned with photos. It was a wonderful antidote to our tense visit – pictures placed by parents who knew precisely what we were feeling. On the left-hand side of an A4 sheet, you would see a picture of a tiny newborn in an incubator, restrained by wires and tubes. On the right-hand side, that same child, now a healthy, cheeky toddler, splashing in mud – these were the children who'd made it, the vast majority of former patients of Unit 8. The concept was brilliant in its simplicity – before and after. It was hope. Those pictures helped to get us through the nervous coffee after leaving the hospital and the silence of that night when lost in our own thoughts.

By the second week, Prof McAuliffe was becoming firm in her view that an emergency section would be required sooner rather than later. Much to her chagrin (she had plans for the weekend!) Flor was admitted to hospital on a snowy Friday afternoon. As one experienced consultant, with a dry wit, quipped: "I don't want you going up in smoke on my watch!" It was also time to prepare James's sisters, Aisling and Isabelle, for the fact that their longed-for brother wouldn't be coming home just yet. And they would have to understand that, for safety reasons, it wouldn't be possible to visit him in the hospital. The only visitors allowed in Unit 8 are the parents of the babies.

In the event, things happened quickly. Having taken the week off work, but feeling pretty useless in the hospital, I had temporarily taken refuge in the cinema. That's when I got the call from Flor. Within an hour, I'd gone from the movie theatre to the operating theatre – and we had starring roles in this production. Apart from feeling silly in my blue shower-cap and plastic shoe-coverings, I was also on edge. We'd been warned that it was unlikely we would hear any cry from our baby on delivery. In fact, for his safety, it was likely he'd be whisked away rather than even shown to us. As I walked in, I thought: *we won't hear him and we won't see him.* The large number of medical staff on hand added to the tension.

But then I sat by Flor, who was cool as a cucumber. It was time to stop thinking about "maybe" and focus on my very limited supportive role in this medical drama. I could clearly see only her and the anaesthetist, because the main event was taking place behind a screen. A matter of minutes later, James Daniel MacCarthy Cunningham was born, and to the relief of everyone in the room, he let out a roar. Minutes later, tightly wrapped in a blanket and little stripy cap, he was carried over to us and told to give us a kiss. The tension in the room evaporated. Conversation flowed between the medics about the problems of commuting between Dublin and Kildare. I thought to myself: "If that's all they're worried about – phew."

After making the relieved phone-calls to family and friends, I was allowed to visit James in the ICU. Back up the stairs. Back through the controlled doors. Back along the corridor. But, this time, to see my son in a place which would be his home for the next 35 days.

Unit 8 is a world apart. It differs in lots of ways from other parts of the hospital, but the main difference is the near silence. Vacuum cleaners are banned, to ensure the babies don't become upset. Instead, the floors are swept. On the wall there's a big plastic ear which, if a sound is too loud, will flash red. These amazing babies are also light-sensitive, so you see some lying there wearing tiny sunglasses.

A baby is defined as being premature if born before week 37. For most of the time, they sleep in incubators draped in covers to reduce stimulation. In effect, it allows the children to do what they're supposed to do – grow. Even their little beds, inside the incubators, are moulded into nests so as to restrict movement – a replication, as much as possible, of the womb they unfortunately had to leave. Parents are encouraged to stroke their babies, or whisper to them – but not to do both at the same time, as this could mean over-stimulation!

In Holles Street, the ICU is divided into three sections. The first is for babies whose condition is critical. Thankfully, James was admitted to section two, as he was able to breathe without the aid of a ventilator. He was born after 33 weeks and weighed just over two pounds (1.32kg). However, some children survive after just 24 weeks' gestation, and weigh in at just one pound. Every eight to ten years, medical advances are able to increase the survival rate by an extra week. However, the younger the baby at birth, the more prone they are to problems later on, such as delayed speech development and poor concentration.

When I sat down beside his incubator, James looked tiny. An assortment of wires linked him to a machine which monitored his vital signs and regulated the temperature in the incubator. But as I scanned the room, it was clear to me, in those initial seconds, that he was bigger and stronger than many of the others. Some of the other babies seemed far more pink – an indication that they'd been born earlier, and their skin perhaps wasn't yet waterproof. In some ways it's a terrible thing, but my confidence in James's chances was formed on the basis that he was clearly doing better than many of the other 35 kids who can at any one time occupy the ICU.

The first time Holles Street designated a unit specifically for premature babies was in 1937, following on from the French identification that "premmies" needed to be nursed under special conditions in order to monitor their temperatures and nutrition. This was reinforced by British advances in specialised staffing. Incubators were in common use from the 1950s, although a problem with too much oxygen led to some children suffering from blindness. Another major leap forward came following the tragic death of Patrick Kennedy, second son of US President, John F. Kennedy. Patrick was born five weeks prematurely and died just two days after being delivered by emergency section. His father subsequently instructed US scientists to focus on assisting prematurely born children. By the 1970s, Holles Street was part of the international movement providing specialised care from specialised staff for these special kids. In 2006, we were the lucky benefactors of that scientific development.

In the course of our baby's first night, two big things happened in his little life. He got to meet his mother properly. I remember her chuckling to herself that her son might pretend not to know who she was, given her less-than-stylish maternal dress-code. Secondly, he was inducted into the special world of "kangaroo cuddles". According to doctors, the instinctive reaction of mothers meeting their premature babies is to gently stroke their backs with an index finger. The next step is to increase the skin-to-skin contact – the mother lies the sleeping baby on her chest, in order to relax the child and help the two of them bond. James got the first of many kangaroo cuddles that night. Later we captured some video footage for Aisling and Isabelle of their little brother so they could see what he was like.

And so this became our new reality. We spent our time travelling in and out of the hospital as James made slow but steady progress – literally, ounce by ounce. Flor would spend her days there, only to come home some evenings and ask me to drive her back in to kiss him goodnight. Again!

The aim of the medical team was to push him up from just over two pounds to three pounds. After reaching that weight, he could be moved to section three, what's sometimes called the "growing" section of Unit 8.

After two weeks, James was moved, as were several other babies – a conspiracy by the wonderful Unit 8 nurses to surprise the "mamas" on Mother's Day. Now that he was well on the way to being sent home, we were assigned a "discharge nurse", who was able to help us plan for life outside the hospital. Prior to the creation of such a post, a lot of children were re-admitted within days – because parents, and indeed some GPs, were too apprehensive to take any decisions.

James came home 35 days, three hours, and 20 minutes after being born. By now we thought he was huge (four pounds!) but soon realised that not everyone thought so. When we offered family and friends the chance to hold the new baby, they would often shy away – too scared of hurting this tiny person. His sisters, on the other hand, were delighted to finally meet and get to know him. Santiago, Jim-bob, Jamie, was finally home.

As weeks turned into months, we switched hospitals; no longer the NMH for newborns, our little boy now attended Temple Street Children's Hospital. For checks on his eyes, hearing and kidneys, he remained under the care of his wonderful paediatrician, Dr John Murphy. And he still does. From the start, the way he manipulated James reminded me of Jimi Hendrix playing his Fender Stratocaster guitar – it was effortless. What's more, James seemed to realise he was being checked out by an expert and would effectively "offer himself up". There would be few complaints as he was flipped, turned about and moved. Even now, playing "doctor" is one of our son's favourite games.

James is now about to turn three years old. He's as tough as any of his friends and taller than a lot of them. He loves swimming, climbing, digging, dancing, cars, Sponge-Bob and his sisters. In that order. For me, his journey from delicate birth to robust boy has taught me two lessons. The first is just how quickly things can change – from normality to emergency. The other is a reminder of the kindness of strangers. The wall of photographs outside Holles Street Unit 8 exists because anonymous parents wanted to celebrate the life of their babies, but also to offer hope – to say to parents like us, at a time of real fear: I know what you are going through and in all likelihood it's going to be okay.

My New Year resolution? To pin up a picture on that same wall of James in his much-loved Spiderman outfit. Beside it will be that frail tiny tot, with translucent skin and no eyelashes yet. We hope to make our own small contribution to that "wonderwall" in Holles Street. To say thanks to all who work there and to all those who find themselves about to visit their new baby: don't be scared. Hang in there.

Paul Cunningham is RTÉ's Environment Correspondent and author of Ireland's Burning: How Climate Change Will Affect You *(Poolbeg).*

Reasons to be Cheerful,
1-2-3

Ian Dempsey

Okay, here goes. I'm alone in the kitchen – "One . . . two . . . three . . . careful . . . four . . . concentrate . . . five . . . nearly there . . ."

In walks my wife, Ger. "Tomorrow is bin day, isn't it?" I'm obsessed with bins. But I couldn't answer.

"Six . . . seven . . . was that six *in* or six *about to go in*? No, I've lost it. I'd better start again. One . . . two . . . three . . ."

Getting the exact amount of baby milk formula from the tin into the newly steamed bottle was a precision art that needed full attention, a steady hand and no interruptions. Putting out a bin was never as intricate.

I really thought I was a busy person until our first child, Shane, arrived on a cold January afternoon in 1990. From that moment, I wondered what the hell I had been doing with my time. He completely took over our world with his toys, clothes, changing bag and steriliser.

In his first year, the novice parents that we were took him on a trip from Dublin to Cork, a road we had travelled many times before as a couple to spend lost weekends at the Jazz Festival or go to a gig in the city just for something to do. You know the usual, a few drinks, a great concert and then maybe something to eat before heading back to the hotel – whenever we felt like it. Total freedom.

This time it was very different. Now, every second was his and every inch of the car was taken up with his stuff. There were things we always brought with us that just weren't necessary anymore. There was no point. We made our merry way down the N7; I drove, Ger had a portion of the passenger seat and all the rest was Shane's. Looking back, it was a great holiday but a massive culture shock.

I suppose we covered all the angles by bringing everything we could possibly need, just in case. As each of our three children came on the scene we'd get a bit more savvy about this and gradually reclaimed some of our own space. Then, as they grew bigger, they took it all back again with games, footballs, guitars and the like.

Shane never slept at all – and when I say never, that was exactly the case. Personally, I believe that he was just keeping a watchful eye over his territory so we understood in no uncertain terms who the boss was. Every now and again he would nod off for a few minutes, but there were no long stretches for the first 18 months or so. His aptitude for "staying up" was more than likely the reason why he walked perfectly when he was only eight months old. By the way, he's now an adult and is catching up on his sleep very well, you'll be glad to hear.

Just after Shane was born, the nurse announced that she was going to get tea and toast "after all that hard work". I thanked her, looking forward to something to eat and a hot cup of tea. She gave me one of those "you really are pathetic" looks and told me that she wasn't talking to me. That put me in my place and it was a valuable lesson I'll never forget.

I suppose before I go any further I should get the name-drop out of the way – Bruce Springsteen once told me when I asked him about children and what kind of a parent he was that as far as he is concerned, "they don't do what you say, they do what you do" (even his conversation has a rhythm to it). This was early in my parenting days, so it has stayed with me as my own children have grown up. It's quite true that no matter how often you say something, the real message gets through with your actions. I mostly do my best.

A couple of years later, when we got used to our new regime, we tried the hotel thing again, this time going to Carrickmacross in Monaghan. At this stage, Shane was talking a lot to virtually anyone who would listen. He had also begun to ask a lot of questions which, when we answered them, would normally be followed up with the supplementary "why?" just to keep us on our toes. He was cursing a lot too, which wasn't really part of the plan. This was all Roddy Doyle's fault. *The Commitments* was the big film on video at the time and Shane had progressed to it from a much more sedate *Winnie the Pooh*. Although it wasn't great for a three-year-old to be effin' and blindin' out of him, I must admit it was quite funny.

Shane, on this occasion made friends with the two musicians playing in The Nuremore Hotel's bar where we went for a drink after dinner. We kept an eye on him and he seemed to be having great fun in front of the stage watching them sing. The night wore on with song after song giving the place a great buzz – until we heard the opening chords of "Mustang Sally" coming out of the speakers. "Shane, listen, it's your favourite song . . . Shane? Shane!" We couldn't see him anywhere but there really was no need to shout – there he was with a determined look on his face, microphone in hand, in his Tigger pyjamas, singing the opening lines of the song at the top of his voice. He gave it welly. They all cheered loudly when he finished, and they cheered again, but this time more politely, when he did his encore, "Achy Breaky Heart".

"That's one, two, three, four . . . is that four or five nights in a row that he didn't wake up at all until the morning? Do you think he's okay?"

Evan was a different story altogether. He literally slept like a baby and ate his food at the right times too. He laughed a lot and it seemed like he loved Elvis Presley from day one. What more could you want? He couldn't have been any more relaxed.

My theory is simple – and I know it can be very dangerous for men to make comments about how easy a birth was for a woman, but I'm going to risk it anyway. It was November 1993 and Evan arrived in Mount Carmel Hospital, Dublin, in what can only be described as a very sociable atmosphere. Ger was all ready to go, the nurses were waiting for the moment, I was there all set to be "a support", or whatever it is that dads are supposed to do on these occasions, and the obstetrician was on his way.

While we waited for him, we started telling jokes and having a laugh. I can't remember any specific story at this stage but one of them was particularly funny. The nurses giggled away in the background and their infectious laughter (infectious in a good way, I should point out) got us all going – including Ger. One minute she was just lying there and the next she was about to give birth. Within seconds and with what seemed like very little effort, out popped Evan James Dempsey into a world that was having a laugh and waiting on him to join in.

We holidayed in Portugal a lot when Evan was a baby and in 1995 we stayed in Vilamoura, beside the beach.

One of the things that he loved was being thrown up in the air and caught again. Simple, but effective. I was pretty good at that (it's great to feel useful) and he laughed out loud every time. But do not try this at home, and I'll tell you why.

On the first day of our holiday, I tried a new technique, in which I threw him up and moved backwards at the same time, adding to the ultimate thrill. He was beside himself with joy. Up again and back again, over and over. He couldn't get enough. "Again, again," he screamed.

There was a problem with the design of the apartment: the ceiling was higher in one area and lower a bit farther back. So, it was up and back – giggles – up and back – raucous laughter – up and SCRUNCH . . . I heard a squelchy sound as his head hit the ceiling and then a scream of shock.

Day one of the break and I'd ruined it all. We hadn't even unpacked. We had just about seen the pool from the balcony. I think the sun even went behind the only cloud in the sky at that very second.

But Evan saved the day when, within about five minutes, he was completely fine. "Again, again, Daddy."

We checked him out and, although there were no lasting effects, this little hiccup could explain why he wanted his blonde hair dyed jet black at about the age of four. It was an Elvis thing and he was serious. This wasn't just for a few days. This was permanent. We bought a black wig in a party shop and got him to try it on, hoping that he'd change his mind. He loved it. He wanted us to make that appointment and change his look forever.

At the very last minute, in one of my many Elvis Presley books, I found a photo of a young blonde Elvis smiling into the camera, which convinced him, for a while at least, that his makeover was a little premature.

"One for the money, two for the show, three to get ready . . ."

One of my favourite places to visit is Doolin in County Clare and, in 1998, this was the scene of the inaugural Lazy Lobster Race where, at the end of the day, there were no real winners. Our friends from Clare, the Garrihys, invited us to stay in their cottage and one afternoon two "live" lobsters arrived for the big race across the kitchen. The children were delighted with the idea and Evan took bets on which one would cross the finish line first. They even gave them names.

It wasn't so much a whistle start, more a push start, but they got moving to the best of their ability, with Terry, the more athletic-looking one, going straight for glory, while Gerry tended to veer slightly off to the left, probably because of an earlier sporting injury. It was almost as exciting as the Olympics, with the children screaming their support for the runners while, at the same time, being careful not to step on them.

In the end, it was Terry who took the honours, with Gerry a dignified second place about two minutes later. After the race, it was suggested that the lobsters were a bit sweaty and probably needed a wash. A steaming hot bath was prepared on the hob and they had a ten-minute soak in boiling water.

Then we ate them.

"Two of those babygros, four of those little all-in-one vests and one of those hats with the bobbin on it, please."

"Which colours would you like?"

"Eh, pink, pink and, yeah, go on, pink, thanks."

All of our children were afternoon babies, which I've always thought was very considerate of them. I mean, I was always up at the crack of dawn for work and wrecked by about 8.00 every evening, so it fitted very nicely into my day.

Aislinn was born on a beautiful sunny day in June 1996 and there was great excitement because she was our first girl. From the moment she arrived, you could see all the future plans being made in Ger's eyes. What she would wear, where they would shop, how they could compare nail varnishes, lipsticks and handbags. It was all very girly and has continued that way ever since.

Ger had been in hospital for a couple of weeks when Aislinn arrived, so the two boys were missing her. I organised to bring them there one afternoon to see her and meet their new sister.

There was massive excitement as we approached Mount Carmel, laden down with presents all round. They asked if they could stay there for hours and hours until it was dark or if the doctors would mind if they slept there so they didn't have to go home again. Perfectly reasonable ideas from two children but unfortunately neither option was possible on the day. They hugged Ger, delighted to see her again, and they were allowed to hold Aislinn too.

After about an hour, I had to break it to the lads that we were going home and that they would be separated from their beloved mum yet again and all because of that pink blob of a sister in the corner, who couldn't even talk or walk. Almost as if they had rehearsed it earlier, they went into hysterics in unison and proceeded to raise the roof. Down the corridor towards the lift and still the sobbing continued. Inside the lift and the noise was beginning to get embarrassing. Panic began to set in as I remembered that we were in a hospital and people might be trying to sleep.

There was only one thing for it. The magic word was needed. "McDonalds?" All was quiet as we headed for the Nutgrove Drive-Thru.

Aislinn is a bit of an all-rounder when it comes to talents. She can sing and dance. She loves languages and is great at maths. She always thinks of other people too, like when she pretends that she enjoys watching football on TV with me.

She's also brilliant at weighing things up and has great powers of persuasion.

One example: we had absolutely no intention of ever getting a dog in the house, yet we ended up with one. In an act of very skillful negotiation by Aislinn about three years ago, we were talked into getting a little white Bichon Frise called Lola. Aislinn drew up a list of the pros and cons and convinced us that a dog was the only way to go.

Feeling duped by a child, we found ourselves at the front door of a kennel down near Carlow. The farmhouse itself was a home and a factory rolled into one, with the puppies all yelping in little containers and dead rabbits on the table waiting for collection. For city slickers like us, this was a bit of a shocking sight but I'm sure it's perfectly normal if that's what you do for a living.

Lola was chosen from two hopefuls in a box. The other one was fast asleep so didn't have the opportunity to impress us. We paid over the money and received a fiver back from the farmer as "good luck" money. This fascinated us almost as much as our new dog.

Although I can't swim myself, and I've been "successfully" taught twice, I'm proud to say that I got all three of our children swimming on their own. Aislinn got the hang of it in France when she was about three years old. I kept holding her up and getting her to swim over to me from different distances. She took to it very quickly and was soon trying on her own. I was still nervous about it but let her swim across the pool. No problem to her – off she went back and forth.

She was so good that I went back and got the video camera to capture her new skill forever. If you watch it now, you see her swimming away and saying, "Daddy, I can swim under water too – watch." In she goes, takes a deep breath and starts swimming with her face in the water for about a metre, followed by another metre, then another and another. She was under for what seemed like an age. The video ends with my voice shouting, "Lift your head, ye wagon," my true Northside roots coming out in a moment of panic.

Dads can be a bit mushy with their daughters and I am no exception. As well as the romantic classic "Everybody Knows" by Divine Comedy being our song when she was a little baby, Aislinn and I now have a secret code which we use every day, with numbers instead of words to pass on messages to each other. 1-4-3 means "I Love You" and 1-4-3-3 means "I Love You Too" – but don't tell anybody.

So, what have I learned from being a parent? What are my observations about the journey so far?

Every child is completely different, so you really have to make it up as you go along.

There is nothing that can break the bond between a parent and child, no matter how hard either side tries.

Sometimes, parents worry too much.

The things that your own dad said to you when you were growing up will suddenly begin to make a whole lot of sense.

Some cartoons are actually quite good.

And I've learnt that it's always worth remembering what Paul McCartney once said about his own children: "Make the most of them – they're just passing through."

Broadcaster Ian Dempsey wakes up the nation every day on Today FM. He is married to Ger and has three children Shane (19), Evan (15) and Aislinn (12). He plays social golf and has only achieved two birdies in his whole life.

My Daughter has Diabetes

Anne Dunlop

Maud was eight and she was off-colour.

"I feel tired," said Maud.

I wasn't very sympathetic.

"Stop waking up so early in the morning," I said; since she was born she has woken at six, and has woken her brother and sisters at six, and has woken me at six, and our entire household is up at six every morning, when eight o'clock would do perfectly fine.

Maud didn't argue with me. She didn't even answer.

"I feel tired," she repeated.

She's infuriating that way.

"It's probably her age," said my mother. "It's growing pains. Is she growing?"

"Growing so fast that the weight is falling off her."

But in quite unusual places. Like her shoulders.

And then there was the staring – not quite a trance, just a vagueness.

My friend said, "At least she doesn't scowl at you as if she hates you. My Isabel was the most perfect daughter in the world until she turned eight; now she stares at me all the time, as if she hates me."

Maud was drinking a lot of water. But we'd just moved to live in the Middle East, and it was very hot, compared to Ireland, so that would account for all the water drinking, wouldn't it?

"Don't drink so much before bed, pet," I said.

"But I'm thirsty."

When she wet the bed the first time I was a bit surprised. She is eight after all. But these things happen. People have little accidents all the time. I remember wetting the bed when I was about eight – having a desperate, vivid dream about needing to find a toilet, but being stuck in a church car park, making small talk with an old lady, and the door to the Ladies was locked. And I kept frantically trying to shake off the old lady in the hope that I could crouch down behind a car and relieve myself; I'd even spotted a suitable car at the far end of the car park . . . If only the old lady would stop talking . . .

And then I peed in the bed.

So I changed Maud's sheets and turned over the mattress and didn't really remark on it. The second time it happened I began to worry that she was disturbed about something – suffering a mental anguish – isn't that why children wet the bed in books?

Mummy said, "Of course she's disturbed. What can you expect? You've dragged her halfway across the world to a new school and a new country. She's missing her friends here in Ireland and her family. She's missing me. There'd be something wrong with her if she wasn't disturbed."

I decided not to phone home for a while.

I was trying to get my novel finished. I was up in the middle of the night in my office on the roof of the house, writing from midnight to three. Downstairs on the floor below I could hear Maud's nocturnal ramblings – out of bed and into the bathroom, pee, drink water, back to bed. Sometimes she didn't go back to bed and I'd find her lying three-quarters asleep on the day bed.

I said, "You shouldn't drink the tap water. It's salty. Salty water will only make you more thirsty. I'll leave a tumbler of sweet water by your bed. Drink that."

"But I'll wet the bed."

"Stop worrying about wetting the bed. It's a hot country. The mattress will dry."

Now Maud was trapped in a vicious circle. She was up all night, drinking water; she was exhausted during the day. She was cranky and uncharacteristically brutal to her brother and sisters. She began to cry at the slightest provocation. After her riding lesson, she was too tired to speak. She sat out during netball because she was too tired to play.

And she was freezing cold – quite blue with the cold. She wore a fleece all day in class, when everyone else was barefoot in a t-shirt.

Sometimes it crossed my mind that she must be sick. Once I even thought, "Diabetics drink a lot of water." I'd learnt it in First Aid when I was an air stewardess. The thought flitted out of my brain as quickly as it flitted in. We have no family history of diabetes, except both my grandfathers and they were over eighty when they were diagnosed – Grandpa Dave because he became addicted to brown lemonade and Grandpa Sam because he was eating jam, out of the jar, with a spoon. Maud showed no particular interest in sweet food but in hindsight that was probably because there were no biscuits in the house.

One Tuesday night she came into my bedroom, woke me up and announced, "I think my throat is closing over."

Finally, a symptom I understood! Something I could take to the doctor!

The following morning I told her teacher, "Maud has a sore throat. If you don't mind, I'm going to take her to the GP in the Specialist Hospital. I'm told you don't need an appointment; we'll be back before break time."

When we were waiting our turn, getting Maud weighed and measured, I casually said, "Do you think we should mention to the doctor about how much water you drink? And about how tired you are all the time? And how cold?"

She was having a staring phase; I don't think she actually heard me.

The doctor had all the time in the world for us. He examined Maud's throat and listened quietly while I ran through the list of her secondary ailments. I felt a bit foolish, for they sounded very inconsequential: she drank too much water, she'd wet the bed, she was cold all the time, she'd lost weight . . .

"How much weight?"

I happened to know what she'd weighed in September, when we left Ireland for the Middle East, because we'd all weighed ourselves for a laugh, on the scales we used to weigh our suitcases. The numbers were jotted down in pencil on the inside of my pocket diary.

She'd dropped five kilos.

I said, "And in the strangest places, Doctor; her shoulders, for example."

"Is she breathless?"

I said, "Now you come to mention it, this past couple of days, running up the stairs, she's been breathless . . ." (I didn't know then what I know now, that when your child is breathless, be afraid.)

"Does she have pain in her stomach?"

I opened my mouth to say "Doctor, we've come here with a sore throat, and you've a waiting room full of patients and they're going to lynch me if we take up anymore of your time . . ." when Maud spoke.

"My tummy is really hurting," she said.

Everything that happened next is a bit of a blur. I know the nice doctor calmly tested Maud's blood sugar with a little prick on her finger, which drew blood, and a machine which gave an instantaneous result. He pronounced her blood sugar six times higher than normal. She was sent to the toilet to pee into a plastic cup and her urine was whisked away to the lab "to check for ketoacidosis". The GP seemed to assume I knew what ketoacidosis was. I know now, of course, that it's what diabetic children suffer from, just before they go "pop".

She was made lie down on a bed in the emergency room, in her school uniform, and hooked up to a drip. I texted my mother and Nick.

"Maud's on a drip. Diabetes?"

I realised that my feet were freezing. In fact, all of me was freezing. "You don't need that blanket do you, Maud?" I asked my eight-year-old daughter, who was hooked up to a drip in the emergency room of a Middle Eastern hospital.

"My tummy doesn't hurt as much any more," she said.

When the results came back they told me that Maud had Type 1 diabetes – juvenile onset diabetes. Her pancreas was broken and unable to produce the hormone insulin.

I did biology at school; I remember learning about digestion. Food passes from your mouth into your stomach and then to your small intestine. By the time it reaches the small intestine it has been broken down into sugar. The pancreas releases a hormone called insulin which carries the sugar into the muscles and tissues to give you energy.

Except Maud's pancreas was broken. It wasn't producing insulin. So the sugar was building up in her blood – all dressed up with nowhere to go.

When this happens the kidneys begin to work overtime, dragging the sugar out of the blood and expelling it from the body in the urine. To do this they need a whole pile of extra water, to make all the extra urine. That's why Maud's brain was telling her to drink lots and lots of water.

Some children have such a desperate thirst they drink bathwater.

And the dramatic weight loss? That was her liver breaking down fat reserves (in her shoulders) to give her some energy, except it's not terribly efficient, just an emergency measure, for dangerous things called ketones are also produced which cause a pain in the tummy.

The doctor told me I was smart (or lucky) to get her to the hospital when I did. Some children are in a diabetic coma before they are diagnosed. Or dead.

They told me she was going to have to stay in the hospital for a few days until they got her blood sugar stabilised. They did not want it to drop too quickly. I asked them if it would be possible for me to pop home and get myself a pair of socks and a sweater. And Maud's nicest nightdress. And her teddy bear.

I stopped on the way home to lift cash from the hole in the wall. I couldn't remember my PIN.

At home I quickly phoned my mother, to explain the earlier text.

She said, "Don't blame yourself! You've never given that child a sweet or a fizzy drink since she was born. And all that breastfeeding until you were a bag of bones . . . And you've cooked for her every day for eight years. I remember you standing making stock from scratch when she was a baby. It's not your fault Maud has diabetes."

Until this point I had not thought to apportion blame. Now doubt clouded my mind. Could I possibly have done something wrong, somewhere along the past eight years, to cause Maud's diabetes?

Thanks Mum. And you were only trying to make me feel better.

Back at the hospital, I was taken to Admissions to sign forms and discuss medical insurance. I was having a laugh to myself – "I honestly don't think she needs a room with a sea view! She's eight!"

He was very solemn, the man in Admissions.

He told me, "This is not relevant. Your daughter is being admitted to intensive care."

They don't allow you to wear your nicest nightie in intensive care because they have to stick things onto your chest and attach them to a pile of monitors. And of course there's the horribly painful needle for the drip, stuck into the back of your hand.

I had one of those inserted when I was delivering Maud.

"Hospital procedure," they explained. "Just in case . . ."

Just in case what?

It was the most painful part of childbirth, which is saying something, for the rest was such a nightmare of agony. I remember lying on the delivery table, thinking: *No one dies from this pain, do they?*

"I've got a TV," said Maud. "Can I watch it, please?"

That night Nick stayed at the hospital with her, and I went home to write my novel. But the words wouldn't unravel in my brain. I couldn't get what I was thinking down on paper. It was very frustrating; a numb feeling. I assume that's what writer's block feels like.

Maud is never going to recover from her Type 1 juvenile onset diabetes. It's something she was born with, and something she'll carry with her all her life. It is a life sentence, but, fortunately, not a death sentence.

Twice a day she has an injection of insulin to compensate for her pancreas not producing any. Nick and I give the injections; we learned by injecting into an orange. When she's a bit older, she will inject herself.

She checks her blood sugar level every couple of hours by pricking the end of her finger, and feeding the glob of blood into her blood glucose monitor. If the reading is high, she goes outside for a run around, or she skips; if it's low, she drinks some orange juice.

Our bodies are very sophisticated computers. It's impossible to cheat the blood glucose reading. One stolen sweetie at the wrong time of day, and the reading shoots way up. Tell tale! Tell tale!

We have to wake her up between 11.00 and midnight to make her eat, in case her blood sugar drops during the night and she goes into a coma, and we don't realise.

Apart from the realisation, very little has changed. I was always anal about what the children ate, and regimented about feeding times. Everyone eats the same breakfast, except Maud doesn't get butter on her toast, and I make her an egg-white omelette while the others eat boiled eggs.

We've discovered delicious tuna fish salads in McDonalds, freshly made, and the McSalad comes with a Diet Coke. (She's allowed diet drinks because they don't have any sugar.)

She's an amazing child, the way she calmly and phlegmatically accepts her condition.

She says, "Everyone has their own problems. Isn't my cousin Kathryn allergic to horses?"

My mother flew out at Easter to visit us. She brought Easter eggs for everyone. Maud got a diabetic Easter egg, which we were all invited to sample. We agreed that diabetic chocolate tastes nicer than the real thing.

Anne Dunlop lives in the Middle East. She is the author of six novels and the mother of four children.

The Super Mammy

Niamh Greene

Before I had children, I had a very clear picture in my mind of the perfect parent I was going to be. For starters, I was going to retain my sense of fun and adventure. As a mother, I knew I'd have to be a responsible adult most of the time but that didn't mean I couldn't fling myself onto the bouncy castle with the kids every now and again, did it? Of course, I'd be careful about setting rules and boundaries as well; even I knew that bit was important. So, for example, there'd be no somersaults or risky manoeuvres while bouncing – that would be totally off-limits. There'd also be no jumping off kitchen countertops, no running with scissors and no poking out eyes with forks.

As well as being a barrel of laughs, I'd be really nurturing. Not in an overbearing or scary stage-school mother way, of course. Yes, I'd encourage my children to shoot for the stars and use their talents (which would be too many to count, obviously), but I'd also teach them to be kind and not step on others' dreams on the way. I definitely wouldn't suggest that they injure another child accidentally on purpose in order to land the lead role in the school nativity play, for instance.

I'd be a counsellor and friend and the first person they would turn to in trouble – not that they would ever get into any trouble in the first place, because, in my infinite wisdom, I would steer them away from making any bad choices. And, while I was doing all that, I'd also cultivate a herb garden, grow my own fruits and vegetables and cook delicious, nutritious meals from scratch every day. My Mensa children would be poster-kids for healthy living and I, in turn, would be feted by everyone from Jamie Oliver to Supernanny. I'd be a cross between Ma Ingalls from *Little House on the Prairie* and Nigella Lawson. In short, I'd be a Super Mammy.

It has been more than eight years since my first child was born and there are some days when, very briefly, I start to think I *am* Super Mammy. Okay, so I may not be an award-winning chef (I've got the licking-your-fingers-suggestively bit down pat; it's the baking I struggle with) and I have yet to plant any herbs or vegetables, but there are times I can believe I'm doing a good job. The goalposts have shifted a bit, of course, because these days, meeting my parenting ideals doesn't mean growing dinner from scratch. It means negotiating a whole host of little hurdles with as much good humour and as few calamities as possible along the way.

A good morning, for example, means not forgetting the children's schoolbags. A very good morning means remembering their hats, music and football boots too. If I can accomplish that and everyone is still smiling, then I can start to feel smug and think, for a split second, that I have the measure of this parenting lark. It's then, of course, right when I'm patting myself on the back for a job well done, that a shining example of award-winning motherhood will pop up from nowhere, burst my perfect-parent bubble and remind me, swiftly and without mercy, that just because I can manage a measly task or two without disaster striking, a Super Mammy I am not.

A true Super Mammy is easy to spot. For a start, she's on time – or early – for everything. She doesn't struggle up to the school gates, miles late and red in the face, vexed with the exertion of a morning spent unsuccessfully trying to bribe a child to eat something, anything, before school. She's also never less than impeccably dressed – she wouldn't dream of wearing pyjama bottoms under her coat to do the school run and she never pulls on a hat to hide the fact that her hair hasn't been washed in a week. She's always perfectly groomed – and so are her children. Not for them a school jumper that has never seen an iron or a pair of shoes that are only ever cleaned with a baby wipe in the car just before reaching the school gates. Not for them hair that hasn't been brushed properly or socks that don't match. Super Mammy prides herself on ironing even her children's underwear and polishing their shoes every single night before bed. All her progeny brush their own hair before they leave the house every morning – a habit she instilled in them from toddlerhood. And she couldn't imagine how any mother would let a child loose in mismatched socks. All it takes is preparation. Preparation is key and she, for one, can't sleep easy until everything necessary for the school day is organised and neatly laid out the night before. That prevents delay in the mornings, meaning her children have ample time to eat the organic porridge she lovingly prepares for them from scratch. It is this commitment to preparation that sets a Super Mammy apart from the likes of me (purely a pretender).

Super Mammy is supremely organised. She does not forget which child has a play date and which has a keyboard lesson. She never mislays a child's homework and then bribes that child to tell the teacher the dog ate it. She never arrives at school to find the yard deserted because she didn't read the note announcing a staff training day. She does not have "trouble" with notes. She does not have trouble with anything.

She walks everywhere with purpose, her diligently organised handbag tucked neatly under her arm. This handbag is her portable office, and in it are the tools that allow her perfect existence to operate without a hitch. An endless supply of antiseptic wipes, nutritious snacks and bottled water is only the start of what the handbag can hold. Super Mammy loves nothing more than a pseudo-emergency situation so she can really demonstrate her worth and the extent of her organisational capabilities.

Your child has a nosebleed? Good news! Super Mammy will come to the rescue in a jiffy with an icepack she just happened to have to hand! Your child forgets his lunchbox? Never fear, Super Mammy always makes a spare, just in case. Your child falls and rips the knee of his trousers? Don't panic! Super Mammy has a sewing kit and will carry out an instant repair. (Her new motto for these credit crunch times is "mend and make-do" – she's even learning embroidery in her very limited spare time.)

Super Mammy does not try to keep track of her life by writing notes to herself on scraps of paper and the backs of supermarket till receipts and then promptly losing them. Super Mammy's pride and joy is her to-do list. She keeps one copy in the handbag (in its own special pouch) and a carbon copy on the cork notice-board at home, where an intricate colour-coded system alerts her to any possible hiccup in her finely tuned and expertly timed day. Super Mammy updates this list hourly without fail so she can keep one step ahead of her hectic schedule. She never misses a parent-teacher meeting, forgets to make a child's dance-recital costume or is caught unawares by a school bake sale. She meticulously files past medical appointments in chronological order so she knows exactly when her child received each jab. She does not shove medical receipts into a kitchen drawer and hope they will somehow sort themselves out.

Super Mammy is confident she is prepared for every eventuality. A last-minute birthday invitation? No problem! Super Mammy always bulk-buys greeting cards and an assortment of kids' gifts; she keeps a stash in her boot specially. She does not skid to a halt in front of the supermarket five minutes ahead of a child's party and then race inside to choose a random present. She carries a roll of Sellotape everywhere; she has never resorted to using Winnie the Pooh plasters to wrap gifts. She also keeps spare clothes, neatly ironed and folded in a recycled bag, in the car just in case her child ever throws up on her pristine upholstery after consuming too many sugary goodies while he has been away from her watchful eye. She could not contemplate having to mop up a child's vomit with pages torn from a woman's magazine, and she has never been forced to ask a child to wipe his dripping nose on his sleeve because she always has a pack of pre-softened aloe vera tissues in her purse. She brings her child's borrowed books back on time. She has never received a notice from the library to inform her that if she doesn't return *The Gruffalo* within a week she will have a nice day out in court.

Super Mammy has a herb garden. And a vegetable patch. She never serves her family fish fingers that may be past their sell-by date or tries to pass off spaghetti hoops as vegetables. Instead, she clips wholesome recipes from magazines and involves her child in meal preparation. (Little Johnny just loves to roll homemade pasta!) She does not watch Rachel Bake on TV with a glass of wine in one hand and a packet of crisps in the other. She does not vow that she will cook like Rachel some day. She could give Rachel a run for her money right now if the mood took her. She has been buying exclusively organic produce for years. Actually, she's recently acquired a few hens of her own. (Little Johnny likes nothing better than to collect the fresh eggs every morning.) She does not buy supermarket spaghetti sauce and pretend it's her own.

Super Mammy's child is extra special. Little Johnny slept through the night from birth, smiled at four days, rolled over at three weeks, walked at six months and wrote his first sentence at one year. Super Mammy now enrols him in every available after-school activity to help him reach his potential and she encourages others to do the same because everyone knows children are sponges and it's up to parents to expand their inquisitive minds. Super Mammy floats serenely from one hellish activity to another. She doesn't develop a hunted look or a serious coffee addiction because every afternoon is now filled with a soul-destroying round of never-ending extra-curricular pastimes that suck her soul dry. She relishes the challenge of being in two places at once – especially when flute clashes with violin on a Tuesday.

So, there you have it. All the evidence adds up to one irrefutable, conclusive fact: I am not a Super Mammy and I never will be. I am not organised, I am not focused and I probably never will have a herb garden or a vegetable patch. But I am also not losing precious sleep over it because, luckily for me, I don't have to be a Super Mammy to have Super Kids. And they are what make me Super Happy.

Niamh Greene is the author of Secret Diary of a Demented Housewife *and* Confessions of a Demented Housewife: The Celebrity Year. *Her third novel is called* Letters to a Love Rat. *She lives in County Kilkenny with two Super Kids and one Super Husband.*

When Two Planets Collide

Eight Examples Why Men and Women
Will Always be Planets Apart

Emma Hannigan

The honeymoon was over. The wedding for 200 guests was a memory, and I was still jet-lagged after the flight from St Lucia. Did we fly first class? Jesus, we were lucky to get a seat at all. The plane looked like it had been made of Lego and the seats were so tightly spaced, we were all in crash position without any collision ever happening.

I was bound to feel bad, right? I expected the post-wedding blues. What goes up, must come down and all that. I'd read that book about men being from Mars and women from Venus. Obviously, I know there is a stark difference between men and women. I also knew the bubble would burst. It was all too "blue-birds and roses". But, as I sat in the boardroom, listening to my boss rabbiting on about the accounts, knowing my tan was flaking off by the second, I could feel my head begin to spin. The computer screen of my laptop was beginning to waver in front of my eyes.

85

"Can you excuse me for a moment?" I staggered to the bathroom, and as I spewed all over the side of the toilet bowl, I could feel the cold sweat trickling down my back. Sitting on the tiles, slumped against the bathroom wall, I looked at the side of the toilet bowl and noticed all the yellow streaks of stale urine. Did anyone ever clean these loos? That set me off again. Not caring that every germ in the world was probably festering there, I grasped the sides of the toilet bowl for support and puked like my life depended on it.

Then came my first taste – excuse the pun – of men being from another planet. It was blatantly obvious to all concerned that I was talking to God down the big white telephone and yet I heard my boss's voice outside the door.

"Are you all right in there?"

"Yep, I'm fine, I'll be there in two minutes," I croaked.

Gingerly washing my hands, I made my way back into the meeting, with my hair plastered to my forehead, looking the colour of putty. The smell of the soap made me retch again. The morning passed in a blur.

By lunchtime, I felt marginally better, but found I couldn't eat my sandwich. The smell of the tuna was beyond repulsive. It must have gone off. I hurried out to the deli to grab something else, and then, the most incredible thing happened: I started to cry. Big, sniffly, snotty crying. I tried to take deep breaths and control myself. What the hell was wrong with me? First I was puking, now I was bawling . . . Oh sweet Jesus . . .

No, I couldn't be, could I? It could be a number of things. *Maybe it's post-amazing-honeymoon depression mixed with a tummy bug? Maybe it's a fast-acting brain tumour, which is minute by minute squeezing my brain and making me rather stupid and emotional? Or else I'm pregnant.*

Passing the delicatessen, I rushed into the chemist and, with shaking hands, grabbed a pregnancy testing kit. Running back to the office, feeling like I was doing something illegal, I stashed the kit under my top, looked over my shoulder and slipped into the loo. Of course, the two blue lines appeared rapidly. Not knowing what else to do, I shoved the tester stick up my sleeve and slipped back to my desk. As usual, my phone kept ringing with customer queries. I answered the calls feeling a bit like a robot. I could have been talking to the Easter Bunny himself for all the attention I was giving the conversations. All I could think of was that urine-soaked stick.

I conducted my day in a blur. It was after five o'clock before I managed to open the bag and look at it again. Maybe when I looked at it this time, the second blue line might have gone away?

Nope. It was still there.

What the hell was my husband of two and a half weeks going to say? I'd been on the pill; this wasn't supposed to happen. What if he didn't want a baby? He might leave. He might decide it was all too much too soon and pack his bags.

By the time my hubby got home from work that night, I'd given up trying to be strong and was sobbing hysterically. Still sitting in my coat, with my bag over my shoulder, no dinner cooked, no lights on, no TV on. Just a quivering, gulping hysterical mess, sitting crying in the dark.

"Emma, what's happened?" He dropped his keys on the floor and rushed over to crouch down and talk to me.

"It's too awful, I can't tell you. You're going to leave me," I blubbed.

"What the hell are you talking about? What's happened? You can tell me, darling." He looked into my eyes, searching for an answer.

"I'm pregnant." Fresh tears sprang from the new bucket of emotion I seemed to have taken possession of. Before that day, I wasn't one of those constantly crying women, honestly.

"Is that all?" He burst out laughing. "Why are you crying so much and why am I going to leave? Is it the postman's or something?"

Here was shining example number two of how different males and females of the species can be. Right at that moment, I was at a suicidal point of devastation. He looked very pleased with himself.

"Of course it's yours, but I wasn't sure if you'd hate me and tell me you didn't want a baby." I exhaled and tried to control myself.

"Well, it's all kind of swift, but wouldn't it be so much worse if we couldn't have kids?" By now, he was looking quite smug and delighted with the news. "Looks like all the tackle is in full working order. Sure, having a baby will be a doddle. Think of it as a bit of human recycling." He scrunched his lunchbox like a happy caveman and nodded. Already I was zooming from calm normality to raging fury in 2.3 seconds. My mind was taken over by dark and very nasty thoughts.

MEN! Here am I feeling like the world is ending and all he can do is rummage around in his trousers. I reckoned it was the famous "hormones" everyone rabbits on about. But right at that moment, if I'd had a dagger I would have stabbed him and his bloody, over-fertile toilet parts repeatedly. It just wasn't fair. Why did men get to have all the fun? Us women went through so much with our emotions and hormones and what did the men do? Go to the pub to brag about their "tackle" being in "working order," while we are left to grow a baby. To have it take over our bodies and make us insane, all the while serving as an unpaid taxi driver. If I survived the next nine months, or more to the point, if Himself survived the next nine months, we'd all be doing well.

"We'll be the coolest parents in the world. That baby is one lucky little person to have ended up in your womb. Just imagine, we'll be so great he or she will want to go clubbing with us and everything." He grinned and nodded as he thought of it all. Example number three: men have a fantastic inner confidence. Of course, the reality of it all is that, today, we are already an embarrassment to our kids and they're still in primary school.

By the third month (or the end of the first trimester according to one of the scary books I'd bought) I looked like I was gestating a whale. I became increasingly protective of and entranced with my unborn child. I was bonding and all that, but Christ, I hated the lack of control I had over my own body. I wasn't one of those women who "blossomed". Oh no, I exploded, well and truly. The word "bump" didn't begin to describe me. I had a mountain up my jumper. I doubled in size everywhere else too. My arms were like hams, my thighs were like a sumo-wrestler's, I had three chins. I swear even my head had grown in circumference.

"You still look gorgeous," Himself had kindly lied one night as I sat with my swollen paw-like feet on the coffee table.

Example number four of the difference between men and women. God bless him, I was consumed with every inch I was expanding, and let's face it, we both knew I looked deformed and I'd probably never be normal again. I was also mental with rushing hormones, but he could lie on the sofa and pat my fat leg and fib kindly. A woman would bite her lip and say the wrong thing like, "It'll all be worth it in the end," thus confirming the uncanny likeness to an ogre and making the situation worse.

It was all going okay. I had got used to being a beach-ball with eyes, peeing every five minutes, having heartburn, piles and stretch marks. Then, wham! I was diagnosed with pre-eclampsia at 36 weeks.

"If you could just lie on the couch please, Emma, we'll put a trace on your stomach," said my gynaecologist as he examined a little coloured stick which he'd dipped into a vessel containing my urine. (Why does nobody tell you how much pee is involved with pregnancy? From the offset, it's a river of widdle. You spend your time aiming into small jars.)

"My hands are like paws and I can't fit into my own shoes. My eyes have disappeared into my puffy face and I think I'm going to explode," I told my gynaecologist.

"Okay, Emma, coupled with the protein which is present in your urine, the rise in your blood pressure and the swelling . . ." He poked where my ankle used to live. It was squashy and, like my leg, had been coated in play-dough by a small dyspraxic child. I looked like I'd had a pump shoved up my arse, and the operator had gone home for the weekend, forgetting to disconnect me. ". . . I'm going to induce you tomorrow morning. Can you be at the hospital at 8.00 a.m. please?"

"What? Tomorrow? But I can't do that. It's not supposed to happen, not for a very long time." I knew I sounded like a babbling fool, but the shock was immense.

"Emma, you did know you were pregnant, didn't you?"

"Yes, unless I've swallowed an elephant, I did get the gist," I scowled. I didn't like him anymore.

I lay awake all that night. The fear of the unknown is a terrible thing. Himself slept soundly (well, for short spells, in between me kicking and elbowing him on purpose). Example number five: men are literally able to take each day as it comes. Women go through every possible scenario of what could happen or go wrong.

We arrived at the hospital the next morning, an archaic building that was both foreboding and scary. Once I'd checked in, I was hooked up to a drip, which would "get me going". In my innocence, I thought I was marvellous enduring the needle being stuck in my arm for the drip.

It all went swiftly downhill from there. The contractions started and presented example number six.

"Oh holy God, there's a volcano erupting in my womb. I think there's a very angry alien trying to claw its way out my vagina," I yelled.

Himself looked mortified. "Shush, Emma, there are other people behind that curtain. You can't shout words like 'vagina' in public." Why was he bothered about any of it at this stage? Besides, we were in a bloody baby factory. They were all used to that sort of talk.

"Vagina is only the start of it, I'll shout *aaargh* . . ." A vicious contraction hit me. It was like a wave of rippling thunder, blistering through my abdomen. It silenced my abuse and made me pant and open my eyes so wide I felt like they'd pop out of their sockets.

The horrible waves of pain continued and a couple of hours later I sat back in the bed to try to get more comfortable. That was when the balloon burst inside me. Pinkish-coloured stuff rushed out of me and hit Himself.

"Jesus, what the hell is that?" he looked astounded.

I couldn't help giggling as I looked at him. It was like Niagara Falls; it kept coming. Gallons of manky stuff gushing out and soaking everything in sight.

"I think that's my waters breaking." I got a sudden jab of pain and it wasn't funny anymore.

"Nurse, nurse, my wife is leaking," he screamed as he ran out into the corridor and accosted a student nurse.

From my bed of pain, I could hear her reply.

"That's all perfectly normal, her waters have gone." She stuck her head in the door. "That should move things along for you now, Emma," she smiled.

Perfectly normal! It didn't feel it.

"I've changed my mind," I yelled as the contractions began to rip through me. "The top half of my body is trying to free itself from the bottom half."

"Would you like an epidural, dear?" The nurse patted my arm calmly.

"I'd like heroin, anything! Just stop this. Christ, it's like trying to shit a fridge. It's not natural, make it stop!" I shouted.

"Now, you don't want that, love, you're doing great. We'll move you into the labour ward and the anaesthetist

92

will be along shortly. The epidural is fantastic, that'll help. Meanwhile, just do your breathing and try to stay calm." She smiled again.

"You're doing great, Em." Himself stood awkwardly looking at me. I think this was the moment *he* realised *I* was from Venus. With his goo-stained trousers and the startled-chicken expression on his face, I almost felt sorry for him – but not quite.

The epidural was indeed astonishing. It was like waving a magic wand. I was able to relax; the pain, although still there, had the edge taken off it. As I calmed down a bit, Himself took the baton and ran with the panic instead.

"Can you see your baby's head?" the nurse tried to guide him over to look. I'm not sure what he saw, but whatever it was, it made his face go all greeny-white. His chest started to heave and he began to sweat. In slow motion, he staggered backwards and had to rest his head against the cold hospital wall.

All the nurses and the gynaecologist rushed to revive him. As they were all fussing over him, an almighty urge to push overtook me.

I yelled like a woman possessed. "*I'm* having the bleeding baby here. If he's out cold, just leave him there. There's a person trying to get out my arse here – can I have some assistance?!"

As our son slid into the world, Himself, who'd managed to stand up again, stared in awe.

"Don't put that slimy thing on my tummy," I shouted, horrified. He was a weird bluish colour and covered in what looked like a mixture of Sudocreme and slug-trail slime.

Whisking him away, the nurse wrapped him in a blue blanket and handed him to his daddy.

"Jesus, Emma, he looks like ET. Are they supposed to be this ugly?" he stared at him for a second and then passed him over to me.

Looking at the little scrunched-up face poking out of the blanket, I instantly fell in love with him. God bless him, he was like a peeled alien. If I didn't love him, no one would. But I *did* love him. I felt such a rush of love and protection it nearly choked me.

"Let's weigh him and check him over." The nurse scooped him up and took him over to the side.

"Are you okay?" my husband asked me. I'm not saying I looked my best but Himself looked like he'd seen a ghost.

"I think I'm doing better than you are. Did you not enjoy that?" I beamed at him, full of New Mother joy. He looked utterly traumatised, like he'd been beaten with a large mallet.

"Flaming Nora, that was horrendous to watch. I can't imagine how it must have felt."

He was sitting drinking the sweet tea which was meant for the mother. I had just been through a birth and he was the one being soothed and treated for shock.

"Well, it's all over now," I answered, finding his distress oddly satisfying.

The wonderful nurses had cleaned the baby and put him in a fresh outfit. We both felt more able to have a go at the bonding thing as the baby was nice and fluffy in a brand new white babygro.

"God, he's amazing, isn't he? Can you believe he's ours?" Himself stared at him and gently put his finger into the baby's tiny hand. Our son instinctively grasped his father's hand. "Look, he's holding my hand. Isn't that amazing? He's only a few minutes old and he knows how to do that." Daddy was smitten.

After our families left the hospital that night with Himself in tow – heading for the nearest pub, no doubt – baby and I were left alone.

I spoke to him. "Hi baba, I'm delighted to meet you, finally. You've made me very fat and unattractive, but it doesn't matter anymore."

I drank in his perfect little face, his miniature features and perfectly formed ears. His head was like a little fuzzy peach, with a thin spattering of white fluff covering it. His skin was pink and as soft as silk.

His fingernails and his little elastic-band wrists were so small I was almost afraid to touch them. I placed my finger, which looked like it belonged to a giant, into his palm and his strong grasp pierced my heart. I knew there and then that I would walk over hot coals for him and physically strangle anyone who ever tried to harm my baby.

God almighty, motherhood was exhausting. I remember watching one of those mental people on a Chinese torture reality game show. The top prize was an exorbitant amount of money and it was given to the person who could stay awake the longest. At the time, I watched the footage and thought it looked like easy money. By the time our son was two months old, I knew how that winner might have felt. For the first few months of our son's life, I envisaged a small yellow-skinned man jumping out of my wardrobe and giving me a large cheque in return for the lack of sleep.

Why does no one ever tell you that you turn into a sleep-starved zombie, with eyes that feel like they've been doused with pepper? Never before had I realised how easy it was to fall asleep randomly. On more than one occasion, I woke with a start, in the kitchen, with the baby asleep on my shoulder. Just like a horse, I'd nodded off while standing. It frightened the living daylights out of me, as I imagined him sliding off my shoulder and onto the hard kitchen tiles.

That brings me on to example number seven and another thing that no one tells you about: guilt. Along with the piles, aching, leaking boobs, the whole world falling out your bottom and the saggy deflated balloon thing that used to be your stomach, you get this guilt complex. This terrifying and awful sense that you're doing the wrong thing.

"What if he's not getting enough food? Can breastfed babies die from malnutrition?" I was ringing Himself for about the fifth time and it was only ten in the morning.

"I don't know, why don't you go to the baby clinic they told you about in the hospital?" he tried helpfully. I know he had a job to go to and all that; in our house, he was the wage earner, so I was left holding the baby – literally. But how could he just go to work and not have that enormous invisible guilt monster breathing down his neck, every step he took?

I went to the mother-and-baby group and was surrounded by earth mothers in stripy tights and denim pinafores, with natural-looking (grey) wiry hair and scrubbed faces. None of them seemed to be bothered by the fact that they hadn't slept for more than a two-hour stretch, since giving birth. All I wanted was to meet a like-minded mother who looked as ashen-faced and shell-shocked as me. I know it's not overly neighbourly of me, but I needed to meet someone who was either on a par with me or, if I'm honest, someone who was coping even worse than I was.

"I just love the bonding and the closeness of breastfeeding. I can't imagine not doing it anymore," said one woolly-jumpered person with a little blonde girl (who could walk, and had teeth) attached to her very droopy breast.

I was only a couple of weeks into the breastfeeding thing and was already wondering when might be the right time to move him onto bottles. I was obviously not an earth mother. I was totally dedicated to my child but I had a problem with a child being old enough to lift his own mother's top and ask for a feed.

After that day, I decided I would muddle along on my own and hope to God that the baby survived his first year. The only thing I knew I had in my favour was the fact that I loved motherhood more than anything else I'd ever done in my life. In spite of the sleep deprivation, the joys my little boy brought to me by far outweighed the bad bits.

Less than a year after that, I became pregnant again. As I had given up work to stay at home with our son, I figured I might as well have another baby. Himself wasn't so sure. Example number eight: most men don't have a loudly ticking biological clock.

"We're doing fine now. The baby is getting a bit bigger and all that. The other thing is, I don't know if I can face another pregnancy and birth." He was wringing his hands.

"In case you haven't copped it yet, it's actually the *woman* who gets pregnant. Not having a womb might make it a little tricky for you to do it. If you feel that traumatised about the birth, then you don't need to come in. I don't mind. I'll just make you suffer for the rest of your life," I smiled sweetly.

It took a bit of gentle persuasion to convince him we would all be better off with one more person in our family. That little angel was our daughter. Now our family is complete. We've moved past the nights of broken sleep and on to the next stage which involves play dates, rugby, ballet and the constant sound of babbling laughter. Every day my children make me smile. Every day my children teach me something new. Every day I know I am privileged to be their mother. Although I am certain men are from Mars and women are from Venus, sometimes, when two planets collide, they can truly create magic.

Emma Hannigan is from Bray, County Wicklow, where she still lives along with her husband Cian McGrath and son and daughter Sacha and Kim. Her first novel, Designer Genes, *has just been published by Poolbeg.*

Baby Bore

Lorraine Keane

"I have never been so ecstatically happy and utterly miserable at the same time."

I can't remember who told me this quote from a new parent, as I was in the midst of a post-natal, sleep-deprived haze myself, but I completely understood where they were coming from. It goes without saying that children change your life for the better; I had heard it repeated so often by many parents. They were all too eager to tell me about the many wonderful things parenthood brings, but I hadn't been made fully aware of the effect it would have on my sleep pattern – or should I say the devastating and irreparable damage it would do to my ability to sleep.

The phrase "sleep pattern" must have been devised by a new parent. My sleep "pattern" can only be described as a minimalist, abstract, surrealist pattern with no order, structure or form – a pattern even Vivienne Westwood couldn't make a dress out of. Once, after a particularly bad night's sleep, I complained to my husband that he wasn't helping matters: "You snored all night, were very restless, talked in your sleep and got up twice in the middle of the night" – to which he jokingly replied, "Yes, I slept like a baby." It was probably the first time that particular phrase was used in the correct context.

You have to laugh. No, I mean it, you really do have to laugh; otherwise you will crack up.

If you can learn to deal with the sleep deprivation then you have half a chance of getting your life back to some semblance of normality. You may not have time to read a book, or even read the paper (actually, if you manage to read the Sunday papers before the end of the following week, you'll be doing well), and the prospect of a little bit of romance during those early days (I really mean months) is highly unlikely. But it is very important to try to retain some sort of social life. You need to get out, switch off and take a break from bottles, nappies and laundry. If you have some friends who are parents, then all the better. You can build up a collection of questions to ask over dinner and this time you will actually be interested in what they have to say.

In the years BC (before children), I remember when we'd meet our friends who have children; as soon as they'd begin talking about their children, my eyes would glaze over and I'd go into a trance, nodding occasionally. When you are "in the same place" (or even soon to be) you hang on their every word, with hopes and expectations of finding a miraculous cure for colic, teething and nappy rash. No matter how ludicrous any of their suggestions might seem, you'll buy it, try it and recommend it again to the next wide-eyed and ignorant new mum or dad. It's a rite of passage. Oh, that and the ability to laugh and say, "It's all ahead of you" to expectant parents.

Imparting information is all very well and should be encouraged. It's good to have a support group, a 24-hour helpline, a know-all girlfriend who can occasionally come up trumps when you're clueless. But a "baby bore" is something completely different. A baby bore will talk incessantly about how wonderfully gifted their child is. I remember being out with friends and experiencing first-hand, for an entire evening, the stereotypical baby bore. When we left I turned to my husband and said, "Don't ever let me become a baby bore, will you?" We agreed that we would come up with some sort of a code, maybe just a nod, or a cough, but some warning sign to stop either of us boring any of our friends to tears with stories of, "You'll never guess what little Ella said last night . . ."

I have a friend whose parents entertain a lot and at the beginning of every evening, his father announces that each guest will be allowed a limit of one baby story (or, in their case, it's usually a grandchild story) over the course of the night. If you exceed the limit, you have to do the washing-up. I was so glad to hear that baby bores have been around for generations. I thought they had only recently emerged along with the Abercrombie and Fitch generation.

As an adoring parent myself, of two highly advanced, entertaining, charming, beautiful little girls . . . ahem . . . I am well aware it is difficult not to talk about your children. As they grow and develop, the smallest response seems like the most momentous occasion. Every day with a baby or toddler brings something new and when it happens you just want to share it with anyone and everyone who will listen.

I remember calling in to one of my sisters just after Christmas. As we chatted over tea, she changed and photographed her baby girl three times. When I asked her what she was doing, she replied, "The clothes are all presents we got for Christmas and the photos are for the people who bought them". I can completely understand this bizarre behaviour, as I now prefer shopping for my little girls than shopping for myself. I too want to send pictures of my girls in different outfits to friends and family, regardless of whether they bought them something or not.

Generally I refrain from an email blitz, but I do have a good collection of photos on my phone. At a recent overdue reunion with friends I was asked if I had any recent pictures of the girls. My phone has a high quality camera with more memory than I would ever need, so the answer was not "yes", but "how long do you have?" One of the pictures was of our two-year-old, standing on the top of a table in a Chinese restaurant in Paris, singing to a large contingent of the Franco-Asian community. I proceeded to tell the story to accompany the picture. It was cute and funny and led to another picture of her older sister carrying a baby goat (don't ask). Midway through that story, my husband gave me "that look". At first I was confused. Then the realisation of what I had just done, what I had become, slowly dawned on me. I looked around the table and met a collection of sympathetic, almost pitying looks. "I didn't?" I asked. "I wasn't, was I?"

Yes, they all nodded in agreement. It was my turn to do the washing-up.

It is inevitable that we all become baby bores at some stage and it's a wonderful thing to be proud of your children, but try to have a built-in safety net, something to trigger an alarm to stop you from ruining a good night out (for the others, I mean). It is good to get out and enjoy the company of adults again and talk about things other than those that envelop your life.

It also goes without saying that the sacrifices you make, the small changes that are made to your social life, the people you see and how often you see them, are so small that they are insignificant compared to the love, joy and utter fulfillment a child brings to your life. They are your "*raison d'être*".

One last word: Do the soon-to-be or wannabe parents a favour – don't encourage them to read my prose. All of the above is a parent's best-kept secret! As parents, we know children are the greatest gift, a blessing, a miracle . . . and we wouldn't want any prospective mums and dads to delay now, would we?

Lorraine Keane is the main anchor on TV3's XPOSÉ entertainment show. Lorraine is from Dublin and joined the TV3 News team from her position as Manager of AA Roadwatch. She has also written columns for VIP *magazine,* Ireland on Sunday *and* The Star on Sunday *newspapers. Lorraine is married to musician Peter Devlin and they have two daughters.*

The Secret of Happiness

Sheana Keane

Like everyone else, before I became a parent I was looking for happiness. I believed I would find it by creating a family, that the simple act of having children and becoming a mother would lead me to ultimate fulfilment.

I was wrong. Once the bliss of maternity leave was over, the happy hormones of breastfeeding faded away, the clock started again and life got busy, the ability to recapture that feeling of sustained happiness became more difficult.

It is a fact. Happiness is not an emotional state that can be placed upon us by somebody else, even by our beautiful children. The only place happiness comes from is within ourselves. We can catch glimpses of it when our child smiles or is funny, but most of us don't feel it all the time. We are often waiting for the next big event to pour happiness into our lives – the next holiday; a new job; when the kids are older . . .

Children, however, naturally possess the secret of happiness that adults spend years searching for. Leading psychologists and spiritual leaders claim that the secret of happiness is to stop the relentless mental chatter in our heads, to become less goal- and future-oriented and learn to enjoy the journey of our lives, to live in the moment. Children are masters of this art form. Adults have to work at it. We live in a busy goal-oriented society that values material and status success over the wisdom of just enjoying what we have and not looking for more.

As we age, I think our eyes start opening to this fact, and children – if we become aware of their power – can become formidable teachers. To start waking up to the lessons my children had to teach me required for me to first feel overwhelmed, trapped and disillusioned as a parent before I understood that the secret to happiness was right there before me. I just hadn't seen it.

Deepak Chopra has a great saying: "I am not a human thinking, I am not a human doing, I am a human being." For the first few years of parenthood, I had definitely become a "parent doing". I thought I was doing everything right. I loved being a parent; I officially did everything good parents should do: we played, we chatted, we baked and we went to the park. However, if I am honest, while I was in the park pushing them on the swings, my mind was divided. I was half enjoying their laughs and half working out what I'd make for dinner. En route to school, I was usually more concerned with not being late than focusing on my chats with them. My head was constantly in the future.

Then I had a great big wake-up call. I had been with my kids all day, doing all the normal daily things, when my husband came home from work. As I cooked dinner, he lifted them into the air and, turning into a child himself, rolled on the floor with them. As they squealed with laughter, it hit me like a bullet. I had been with them for twelve hours and they hadn't laughed uncontrollably like that once. I was so caught up in the practical things that needed to be done as a parent that I was not sucking the marrow out of life with these amazing human beings.

I was a human doing; I was a parent doing.

The problem was, I felt that I had no time to stop. My children were two and one years old at the time. I had no time to step out of the parenting/working treadmill to truly enjoy my children, my husband or my life. I was too tired, too busy, too distracted.

But this was my life-changing moment and I started to become a human thinking. I started reading and studying a new branch of psychology called positive psychology, which is the scientific study of happiness. In one of their studies, they asked volunteers to keep a gratitude journal every night before they went to bed; in it they were asked to note three things that went well that day and why they felt good. They measured the volunteers' happiness levels before the experiment and again six weeks later. The results were that every single volunteer measured significantly happier after they had kept the gratitude journal for a few weeks. This prompted me to start keeping a gratitude journal myself, but I called it "The Good Day Book".

I have kept it now for a number of years and can safely say the science works. My journal is filled with moments spent with my family and friends: five minutes when I jumped on the bed with the kids, my son's giggle when I tickled him for a few seconds, a great night out with friends. The things that made me feel good each day were never big profound events, they were always small, potentially missed moments. Keeping the journal simply made me notice and appreciate all these happy moments that I already had.

I also began to recognise those moments as they were happening, so that in the park, on the swings, when my son laughs, I catch the moment, I shut out all other thoughts and concerns and try to become present, enjoying the fun he is having. Guaranteed, I get more enjoyment out of these moments than ever before. If they are jumping on the bed, I may be in the middle of chores but I stop just for a few minutes, shut off all thoughts of what jobs I have to get done and get on the bed and jump with them. Of course, there are dinners to make, clothes to be ironed, but when I'm playing with the children now I consciously stop my mind wandering off to worry about this list of chores that in truth never really end anyway. The Good Day Book worked for me – the science is correct, I started to feel happier, to have a general sense of well-being, peace and, crucially, an appreciation for everything that I had in my life. It was subtle but it was profound. I was starting to become a human "being".

I try to apply this approach to every area of my life now – time with friends, a walk on the beach, interviewing guests. It sounds simple but it is actually quite difficult to do and requires practice, and even then it doesn't always work. It is worth pursuing though because when I can manage to shut out all babbling irrelevant thoughts, it helps me to pay attention to the small and often extraordinary or beautiful details that I may have missed before. I now understand why experts say "learn from your children to climb into the moment". I have become a sponge, trying to learn their ways. I study children playing: they are focused on only one thing – climbing up that huge slide and getting their sliding buzz. They are not thinking about homework, or yesterday's argument; they are absolutely in the now. As adults, the relentless mental chatter in our heads (over 80 per cent of which is repetitive, according to scientists) prevents us from enjoying what is in front of our eyes. I don't know when the mind stops living in the now but our children are doing it all the time. When they are playing, I consciously make a decision to copy them and then throw myself 100 per cent into the moment with them, which usually ends up with me climbing up the slide too – we end up enjoying our time together more. It may happen naturally with some people but with me it's a work-in-progress and a conscious effort.

This desire to live in the moment does have its difficulties. It is beautiful while we are watching children play but it clashes with an adult's sense of timing when trying to get them fed, dressed or to bed and working to the external clock. This clash between their free way of life and our clock-bound one is the source of much frustration and causes the most arguments. They want to marvel at the snail while we are trying to get them to school on time; we get stressed and an argument ensues. I started looking at where the problem was and had to admit that their behaviour is consistently the same and, despite my endeavour to learn from them and live in the moment, my ability to do this was dictated by my stress levels, which varied on different days.

Generally on Mondays I was Mary Poppins – marvelling at the snail, making up stories about the snail, painting the snail – but by Wednesday I wanted to kill the snail and felt that every whine and moan from my children was a personal infringement of my human rights. The difference wasn't them – they were always just children – it was my reaction to them. By Wednesday, what I call "groundhog day syndrome" had generally kicked in: I felt like I was doing the same list of thankless, repetitive tasks, day in, day out, all day, every day, for years.

I started assessing when I worked best and enjoyed being a parent and realised that I am at my most fun, patient and interested just after I have spent some time by myself – walking, jogging or reading, it didn't matter what I was doing just as long as nobody was pulling out of me. That time was for tending to myself. I used to think time out was a luxury and not something that was possible for a parent of young children, but I have come to the conclusion that it is a necessity. I realised that I had given all my time to family, work and friends for over two years and had forgotten about myself. I had depleted my reserves, which left me with very little left to give anyone else. A holiday was not the answer – that's only a short-term fix. It became essential to create more time within every week to create a long-term sustainable change.

My husband and I sat down and worked out a formal plan. We now take turns every morning in getting the kids up and out for school. The other has the morning to themselves and can slowly meander their way to work. The golden rule is this: on your morning off, you are not to be disturbed by the children; your time is sacred. Now on the days that I am "on duty", I endeavour to be totally in the moment, paying them 100 per cent attention – and I can, because I am not jaded by the repetition of it all. I can focus on enjoying their wonderful personalities, instead of me making sandwiches while they have breakfast. We all sit down for breakfast together, we chat, I really listen, we feed the ducks on the way to school. We have fun. And, naturally, I really look forward to my mornings off. I go to the local coffee shop, read the paper, go for a jog. We do the same at night, each putting the kids to bed on alternate nights. Again it avoids the groundhog day syndrome and they get patient parents reading them a story every night. The final input to our weekly routine is one night out for us parents. We meet straight after work and chat about life, love and the universe, and then maybe see a film or play – anything, as long as someone else is putting the kids to bed and we are focusing on each other. It's so simple, but it has changed our lives.

Watching how quickly I allowed my life to become a series of activities which took priority over really enjoying the people around me and noticing how my spirit became lost in these activities taught me the importance of regularly stepping out of the world and feeding my soul by spending time in utter silence. Reading, walking, meditating, whatever the activity is, it is vital to my peace of mind, happiness and parenting skills. This may not seem like a huge discovery, but the world can get so busy it can often be difficult to see the wood for the trees. It has become fundamental to me now, allowing me to recharge my batteries, analyse problems rationally or to just appreciate the extraordinary beauty in nature and reinvigorate my soul. Without any sentimentality, I can genuinely say it makes me a better parent and a more thoughtful human being.

Despite my best efforts, however, my children still know how to push my buttons and test my patience, but I am more likely to deal with them in a calm way. I have come to the conclusion that when children's behaviour sometimes needs to be corrected, it can be done in a rational, reasonable, calm way, without resorting to shouting or power games. If I do snap and end up battling them, it is usually because I'm tired, stressed or I haven't had time to myself in a while. I don't blame myself for snapping; I just try to recognise it as it is happening and attempt to make a rational decision as to whether it's their behaviour or mine that needs correcting. If it's me that is stressed, I try to unwind my coiled mind and do whatever is needed to de-stress myself and take my own "time out" as soon as I can. I'm not perfect; it doesn't work all the time, but I think the ability to become aware of behaviour rather than being controlled by emotional reactions is half the battle and this coupled with practice certainly helps. Maybe by the time they are 30 I'll be perfect!

I have changed fundamentally as a human being since having children, mainly because of the challenges that parenting threw at me. Before, I was naive and probably a little arrogant. I genuinely thought I was going to be a perfect earth mother and to find that I was having difficulty and that the workload involved was overshadowing the enjoyment was a huge disappointment to me. But I am so grateful to have learnt the lessons that I have, so early in their lives and mine. The workload is the same but my priorities and attitude have changed. I feel a deep appreciation for all that I have, which I reaffirm every day, and I hope I am a kinder, more attentive human being as a result.

Above all, I realise now that the parent is not the only teacher in this relationship. I have absolute respect for my children's expertise in the art of living to the full and while I have plenty of lessons to pass on to them, I am a humble student of their approach to life.

Sheana Keane is co-presenter of RTÉ's The Afternoon Show. *She lives in Dublin with her husband and two young children, Isabelle (4) and Arthur (2).*

The Love Letter

Cathy Kelly

There are many different sorts of love letters. This one, written for my sons, is almost too complicated to put on paper.

"How big is my love for you?" I ask them, and the answer is "Bigger than the ocean."

They know the answer because I've told them, endlessly.

My job is to write but when it comes to writing about Murray and Dylan, there just aren't enough words to do it justice. Everything I write seems like a cliché. But a cliché becomes a cliché when it's endlessly true. And mother love is the truest of all.

Our worlds collided over six years ago. Pregnant with twins is almost a comedy line by itself, with petite me as the punchline. From the back, I like to think that I didn't really look pregnant. From the front, I looked like one of those "Weebles wobble but they don't fall down" things.

I became used to wearing enormously stretchy clothes and wrenching the fridge open for regular inputs of ice cream.

Pregnancy is a state in itself and when it's your first pregnancy, you almost forget that at some point, children will be born and you'll be in the next state.

That warm summer of 2003, *The Life of Mammals* was getting its first airing on TV and I lay, whale-like, watching echidnas oozing milk and thinking, with a certain contended connectedness to the earth, that humans were mammals after all.

I might move to Newgrange and start planting herbs, I thought, in my Earth Mother haze. Dance in the moonlight, sky-clad.

On a hot July day, my three-stone-heavier self became a mother of twins. Dylan and Murray. Thoughts of growing herbs went out the window. Herbs? I didn't have time to wash.

I instantly understood why mothers can do five things at once: because they have no other option. You cannot loll in bed or spend hours in the shower when two small beings are shrieking at the top of their lungs for you. Well, you can lie there, but the power of mother-love will force you onto your feet.

The doctor had advised a caesarean, as I'm very small, so I was supposed to lie in bed for twenty-four hours once Murray and Dylan had made their arrival. That was the theory. In practice, in the middle of that first night of motherhood, when the lovely nurses in the Rotunda were busy, I realised that me and the drip would have to get out of bed and do something.

Bells bother me. I'd prefer to make my own coffee than call room service, so I decided not to ring for the nurses that night. Instead, I hauled myself out of bed, stood unsteadily over the two little hospital cribs, and got to work.

It was the best thing I could have done. The sort of pain that would have had me whimpering pre-babies was nothing now that I had my own children to nurture. Pain. What pain? I am in charge and something must be done, now. It helped that both boys possessed very strong lungs and roared lustily at the tops of their voices. That sort of blanked out any *"I need to lie down, I've just had surgery"* moments.

I eventually got faster at changing nappies – I like to think I was like one of those Formula One pit-stop tyre changers with fingers awhirl – but that first night . . . oh dear.

The boys seemed so small, I felt so big and my belly – a jellyfish sponge lying under my skin – scared me each time I bumped into the cribs. I was like Mama Whale waddling around, hormones screeching, utterly exhausted. I couldn't sleep – well, I could, but the two new men in my life wouldn't let me. Once one was asleep, the other would wake up. Inside me, they'd worked out a rota. *"You cry first, then I'll come in, right?"*

Pre-children, I'd assumed that I'd still go away on weekends without the children, still live a life outside of theirs. The day they arrived, I realised that this was never going to happen. Go away for a weekend? I wanted their cribs almost on top of my bed that first night, didn't want even an inch to separate us. If there had been room, I'd have put them sleeping beside me, but those hospital beds are scarily narrow.

Every time they slept in tandem – and trust me, it wasn't often – I lay there in a smiling haze. I was tired and sore, but I was their mother.

First-time motherhood has been described many ways. Some people say it's like being underwater for six weeks. Only six weeks? I think it's like being blindfold in a foreign land where you don't speak the language. You are operating on instinct. Your mind is too bewildered to process the information but the limbic brain kicks in. In other words, Mother Nature takes over. Thank heavens for that, because I didn't have a clue.

After six days, dizzy on new motherhood, I left the hospital. I still had the jellyfish sponge belly – who are these women who fit into their pre-pregnancy jeans after a week? – but I was on a high. I was a mother of beautiful, healthy twin sons. I was also pretty anxious about going home with my babies because this whole mother-of-twins business is hard work. However, I comforted myself with the knowledge that if you can breastfeed two babies at the same time within the confines of a tiny hospital bed, without anyone falling out, then you can do anything. You need another person to help with this process, by the way, and body issues tend to disappear when you no longer care that it's someone else's hand squashing your nipple into the baby's mouth. We're mammals, dammit! Get with the programme.

Going home was both wonderful and scary. I had fantasies of lying in the big double bed with a baby snuggled on each side, and me reading happily in the middle. Somebody really should have told me. That sort of thing only happens in home furnishing catalogues.

Despite realising that this me-and-babies-in-bed thing was a mere fantasy, I got more rest because the boys' beloved daddy, John, was there to care for them too. He knew instinctively what was right and in his arms, they were calm and serene. Home was fabulous.

The snag was, there was no nurse on hand to answer all the anxious questions. *"Do you think his left eye should be blinking like that/left leg should be curled like that/should it be that colour? Is that normal?"*

I'm now sure that all babies can be totally different and be normal, all at the same time, but I didn't know that then. Anything in the books was the gospel and anything outside of what it said in the books was clearly wrong. You see, I like to read about things. I'm the woman who brought three books (don't laugh) into the hospital, albeit two of them being baby books. So I read the entire canon of baby books endlessly.

I read about Baby Whispering, Non-Baby Whispering, baby routines straight out of the army handbook, baby routines that were for the laid-back baby; I even got a book about how to get my groove back, although I'm not sure if I ever had a groove in the first place, but still . . .

I was living happily, if exhaustedly, on Planet Baby. And still I felt as if I wasn't getting it right. There was no routine at all. Every morning – a word which implies that there was something that passed for a proper night, and there wasn't – was like being on a rollercoaster. Who knew what would happen today. For someone who could never have forty winks and only slept in the afternoon twice in my entire life, I could catnap anywhere. Let me get horizontal, stick in ear plugs and I could sleep.

Meanwhile, the boys had their own routine, another thing they'd clearly worked out beforehand. *"This Mummy person is great, she's like the Duracell bunny. Let's keep her on call twenty-four/seven."*

It got harder. I was getting more tired and began to understand how sleep deprivation is a form of torture. I was convinced I was getting more and more things wrong. John told me not to panic but I didn't have his calmness about the whole baby world.

How had the human race lasted so long when it was so difficult? Imagine doing this in the desert without baby monitors and a microwave? Where was my lovely Earth Mother, we're-all-mammals vision now?

The difference between us and *The Life of Mammals* is that David Attenborough's versions don't have vast tracts of public opinion on "the right way to mind a baby". They don't have books discussing demand feeding versus whenever-the-hell-you-want feeding. They don't have people delivering gorgeous gifts of clothes you never get round to putting on the children because, let's face it, you're whipping off their babygros every hour, so why bother with little jeans and shirts, no matter how cute. They let the mother learn how to be a mother, whether it's steering her baby leopard around the bush waiting for a stray antelope to come by or a kangaroo knowing that the joey has to stay in her pouch for months before it will be ready to face the world.

I remember the day I got it. I trusted my instinct that one of my sons was sick and brought him to the doctor. Yes, the doctor agreed, he wasn't well.

"I knew it!" I proclaimed.

The doctor explained that medical students are told to listen to mothers who come in with sick children because a mother's instinct is so powerful and often right.

At that moment, something changed inside me. The books were great sources of information, for sure, as was my beloved John, but only I could know instinctively what was right or wrong. Nobody knew my babies better than I. That knowledge was a huge power surge running through me. I could do this. Womankind had been born to do this. What a wonderful relief to sink back into Mother Nature and trust.

Instinct is a wonderful thing. Like the huge whale diving in the ocean with her calf at her side, who has no books to tell her what's right, we do know what the right thing is. Somewhere deep inside ourselves, we have all the tools to be parents.

All you need is the love, and the love of a parent for a child is unfathomable and deep.

Cathy Kelly's latest novel is Once in a Lifetime.

The Growing Years

Mary Kennedy

"You can tell me anything and I will
listen and laugh
or listen and cry
or listen and do nothing at all
except love you –
indisputably,
irrefutably,
infinitum."

JAYNE JAUDON FERRER

I was delighted when I came across these lines in a collection of poetry called *Dancing with My Daughter* by an American writer, Jayne Jaudon Ferrer, because, in a far less poetic way, I've been giving my children the same message since they were very small. It's affirming to know that others have been doing the same thing.

No matter how many baby books and mothering manuals we read, parents realise that all bets are off when the children get that bit older. You have to accept that they have their own personalities, their own needs and their own pressures. That's when we hope they realise that they can tell us anything and we will be happy for them, sad for them, worried for them, but no matter what, we will always and in all ways love them.

A mother's instinct is to protect her children and to do her best for them always. The same is true of fathers and there's a lovely reference to that in one of the Irish novelist, Niall Williams' books, *Only Say the Word*.

> *"I know the harrowing the world has already made*
> *in the soft places of your spirit. I know your fears*
> *and your pains and because I am your father, I*
> *cannot know them for an instant without wanting*
> *to make them pass."*
>
> NIALL WILLIAMS

The hardest thing for a parent is to let go because for so many years when our children are small we're in there beside them, holding them, doing everything for them, protecting them and always watching out for them.

Jayne Jaudon Ferrer has another book of poems called *A Mother of Sons* and there's a lovely piece in it called "Midnight Rendezvous" which brings me right back to the early baby days. Those first days which every mother of a newborn will have experienced . . . even the ones who have those wonder babies who, allegedly, sleep through the night from day one!

"It is with something less than
maternal goodwill that I crawl,
asleep and annoyed,
from my coveted bed
to silence your angry screams
violating the night."

JAYNE JAUDON FERRER

The encounter continues of course until the baby is settled and sleeping peacefully in mother's arms and the poem finishes:

"My last trace of irritation
over interrupted sleep
dissipates in a hug, a kiss,
and a smile.
You will never remember
these midnight moments together;
I will never forget."

JAYNE JAUDON FERRER

And it's true. We never forget. As in this poem, we look back with nostalgia to those baby days but at the time we couldn't wait to see the back of them, as we yearned for a decent night's sleep. I often think it's such a pity that these beautiful bundles of joy come into our lives when we are at our lowest ebb, going around in a state of constant and utter exhaustion, recovering from a birth and suffering from sleep deprivation.

Oscar Wilde said: "It's a great pity that youth has been wasted on the young." You could apply the same logic to babies coming into our lives when we are too tired to genuinely enjoy them. We dedicate our lives to them, nourish, teach and play with them. We give them every opportunity we can but we do tend to be looking to the future a lot – looking forward to when they can feed themselves, dress themselves, walk to school on their own . . . and then all of a sudden they're grown up and in some ways they're gone.

I find myself looking back at baby photos and realising that I had no notion of how quickly those years would pass – in a whisper. I'd love the opportunity to have some of those moments back again. I'd love if I could just sit and hold one of my babies' fingers without having to think about the next feed or other chores that had to be done . . . to just be and live in the moment.

While I was on holidays in France during the summer with my grown-up children, I spent time sitting by the pool observing mothers with babies and toddlers. To a woman, those mums were attentive, vigilant even. They walked along behind their children for fear they'd fall, held them in the water and played with them. They gave them bottles and yoghurts and soothed the children when they got tired and cranky. Their own lives were on hold. I remembered being that soldier.

Motherhood is a most precious gift. It's the best thing that's happened to me and I know I'm not unusual in that. From the moment your first baby is born, your life is transformed. There are ways in which motherhood is pure delight.

*"All that I knew of heaven
I saw in my babies' eyes."*

EMILY ORR

Those lines are from a poem called "The Witless Mother" by Belfast poet Emily Orr. Let's face it, there are ways in which we become witless when we have a baby. I know I did. For a full six weeks after I had my first baby, I felt totally overwhelmed, I was exhausted and tearful. There were days when I was still in my dressing-gown at tea time. I just hadn't had the time to get dressed. That's difficult to accept when you've been totally in control of your life up to that point. And because this is your first experience of motherhood, you don't know when this feeling of helplessness is going to end. You can't see the light at the end of the tunnel. There's no doubt that there are ways in which motherhood is difficult.

> *"Lord, thou art hard on mothers:*
> *We suffer in their coming and their going;*
> *And tho' I grudge them not, I weary, weary*
> *Of the long sorrow — And yet I have my joy:*
> *My sons were faithful, and they fought."*
>
> PADRAIC PEARSE

Now I'm not suggesting for a minute that Padraic Pearse's poem "The Mother" is a typical example of the challenges of modern motherhood. It was, after all, written in 1916, at the beginning of the last century. This mother was about to lose both her sons to execution. There are, however, depths of maternal feeling here that are universal: the weariness, the sorrow and the joy. Mothers worry all of the time: Is my child healthy and happy? Am I passing on the correct values? Are my children listening? These words echo all mothers' concerns:

"Have I taught you the right things,
my darlings?
Between laundry and table-setting,
Ironing and pants-hemming,
Manners and morals and
Where to pin the corsage,
Did I remember to teach you about love?
About listening and hearing
And holding and helping."

JAYNE JAUDON FERRER

There are times, as we travel along the path of motherhood, that we need reminding that we are very lucky and privileged to have given birth. No matter what worries or anguish we feel as mothers, we must remember that. I came across a quote while I was at a post-natal low ebb years ago and I cut it out and kept it.

"Think always, that having the child at your breast
And having it in your arms,
You have God's blessing there."

ELIZABETH CLINTON

It's a very simple thought. I know I didn't fully appreciate Elizabeth Clinton's meaning at the time. I simply used it as an encouragement to keep me going in those exhausting days. But I fully understand the truth of it now and I cherish the memory of those early baby days, sleepless nights and all, which pass so quickly by.

We all want the best for our children and we all want our children to be the best. I don't mean "best" in a competitive or academic way. We want them to be the best of people – people who are honest, fair, compassionate, loving, happy and healthy. The list of qualities is endless. As I was saying, when they get older we see their personalities develop and we have to accept that they are their own people. Listen to the words of Kahlil Gibran when The Prophet speaks of children.

"You may give them your love but not your thoughts,
For they have their own thoughts.
You may house their bodies but not their souls,
For their souls dwell in the house of tomorrow, which
you cannot visit, not even in your dreams.
You may strive to be like them, but seek not to make
them like you.
For life goes not backward nor tarries with yesterday."

KAHLIL GIBRAN

All of a sudden comes the moment when they start to spread their wings, to socialise with friends and to want to do things their way. Sometimes their way is not our way but we have to respect their individuality and desires.

The words of the nineteenth-century American poet and philosopher Henry David Thoreau come to mind:

"If a man does not keep pace with his companions,
Perhaps it's because he hears a different drummer.
Let him step to the music he hears,
However measured or far away."

HENRY DAVID THOREAU

I love those lines. They're open, magnanimous, gracious and show an acceptance of difference and of alternative lifestyles. They are a salutary lesson in these days of the Celtic Tiger when so many people seem hell-bent on making more money, on buying bigger cars and houses and on running themselves into the ground.

I suppose the lesson for mothers is that we have to let go, to allow our children to move on and away from us and be their own person, secure in the knowledge that we are always there for them, that we love them and that we know them intimately.

Patrick Kavanagh gives a lovely reminder of the innate knowledge a mother has of her child in his poem "In Memory of My Mother Died 10 November 1945".

"You will have the road gate open, and the front door ajar
The kettle boiling and a table set
By the window looking out at the sycamores . . .

You will know I am coming though I send no word
For you were lover who could tell
A man's thoughts – my thoughts – though I hid them
Through you I knew woman and did not fear her spell."

PATRICK KAVANAGH

There's nothing more sure than that a mother's instinct is very strong when it comes to the person she has carried in her womb for nine months and then cared for through baby, toddler, child, adolescent, teenage and young adult years.

We give our children unconditional love and support, with the wisdom and experience we have garnered in life. We hope, as in Patrick Kavanagh's case, that through us, our children will get a knowledge and an understanding of the world and its people. And as they grow up and move away, we will, like Kavangh's mother, always have the gate open, the door ajar and the kettle on.

And we hope that as adults they will feel towards us the love and the warmth that another Irishman, John O'Donohue, displays for his mother Josie in his beautiful poem "Beannacht" (Blessing).

> *"And when your eyes*
> *freeze behind*
> *the grey window*
> *and the ghost of loss*
> *gets in to you,*
> *may a flock of colours,*
> *indigo, red, green,*
> *and azure blue*
> *come to awaken in you*
> *a meadow of delight."*

JOHN O'DONOHUE

What I like about those lines is the understanding on the part of the son that as time marches on and children become adults, parents feel a sense of loss. There's an inevitable sadness, a greyness and a loneliness involved in this process. He knows this and wishes for colour and delight to be a part of his mother's life at that time.

The poem finishes with a warm declaration of love and protection.

Mary Kennedy

"And so may a slow
wind work these words
of love around you,
an invisible cloak
to mind your life."

JOHN O'DONOHUE

Wouldn't any mother be delighted, after all her years of rearing and caring, for her child to feel like that about her? *(Extract from* Lines I Love *by Mary Kennedy (Merlin Publishing, 2007) reproduced by permission of Merlin Publishing.)*

Mary Kennedy is a TV presenter with RTÉ. She worked as a newscaster, has presented a variety of programmes on television, including the Eurovision Song Contest, Open House *and* Up for the Match *and is now co-presenter of* Nationwide. Lines I Love *is her second book. She published a memoir,* Paper Tigers, *in 2004.*

The First Leg

Sonya Lennon

It's 4.30 a.m. I'm awake, twisting with anxiety and annoyance over a stupid work incident. How could someone who claims to value my work have said those things – and not even to my face? And it had to be retold to me by a photographer. You think you know someone. Stupid bastards. That's it, never again. You give body and soul to these people.

And I think I'm pregnant.

Well, I won't be giving my service to them again; wouldn't mind, I practically do give it. Might as well do it for free. Why is it always the little clients, who pay the least, that cause the most pain?

I am definitely pregnant.

Right, that's it. There's a test in the bathroom, I'm bloody doing it.

Right.

"Honey . . . Honey? . . . Baby, I'm pregnant."
"That's great Baby, we'll talk about it in the morning."

So, ten years into a relationship with a man I love, who loves me, we decide we'd like to try to have a baby. Why now? What makes this the right time? We have the love, and now we have our first home. The minute I saw it, I knew, a bit like the man. A beautiful Victorian house which heaved like a bosom, brimful of grandparents, foster kids, kids and basketball hoops. It was cluttered and partitioned like a warren, a million miles from our dream aesthetic, but the potential was there.

It had space, glorious space, holy grail of the city dweller, particularly those of limited budget. It was in an up-and-coming, down-and-dirty area. Fine by me. Ever since I moved out of my cushioned middle-class family home, I've lived in funny spots, quirky neighbourhoods with character and soul. I wouldn't know what to do with myself in some leafy avenue. I like down and dirty.

We started phase one of our grand plan by ripping out the chintz and stripping back to white and wood. Clarity and space.

Let's get a dog. Great idea. And what a great dog, a monstrous cartoon character of a beast, pure white with one grey ear and amber eyes. We loved that dog. Four stone of Staffordshire bull terrier who thought she was a four-pound chihuahua.

Two things happened: I walked the dog and I mothered the dog. A year later, I was physically fit and psychologically ready to consider becoming a mother. Luckily, I wasn't on my own.

We were pretty sure we had got a lot of love to give. But in fertility terms, we were just entering the "not so clever" phase. I was 36. Well, that's us, selfishly busy having a great time for ten years, dancing on rooftops, laughing and crying and falling over. Our whole gang were happy-go-lucky party folk, all of the same vintage, all in the same boat. Great friends. I love my friends and not everyone can say that.

Some great friends had starting having babies, and that's how it begins.

It's not envy or keeping up, it's just hardwired, for all but the unusual few. I know a few of the unusual few and I like them. I like their sense of freedom and clarity, their independence. Frankly, it doesn't seem odd to me to decide not to have children. There's something fantastically urbane and intellectual about that choice. But I always saw myself as a mother eventually.

The family that created me was joyous and loving, my parents an inspiration to any parent. I am one of two children, my extraordinary sister being six years my junior. Of course, every family has good times and bad, but the general philosophy of enthusiasm and mutual respect worked. I always said I'd like two children; I guess normality is what you know. And whatever works, works.

Like everything in our lives, myself and Dave discussed and dissected the decision to try for a child, before taking the plunge. We are not control freaks, but we're both big fans.

Well, I think we're ready, but that doesn't mean it's going to happen. There are no guarantees. The thing about it is, we're really happy, we love each other, we love our life together. Deciding that we want a child and finding out we can't have one; now that I wouldn't like.

We were both terrified. Imagine finding yourself frantically chasing something that you weren't even sure you really wanted. A nightmare loop of expectation, medical prodding and procedures. No thank you.

So let's give it a little shot and see what happens. No panic if we don't crack it; we'll have fun trying. Nice and loose.

"Honey . . . Honey? . . . Baby, I'm pregnant."

I knew pretty much immediately. I burst out crying and bawled inconsolably with the sheer abandon of it. All those years of trying to stay unpregnant have a firm hold on your psyche.

Five days later, myself and my darling friend Catherine, a recent mother, did the cliff walk in Howth. As the wind whipped around the Head, my nipples pulsed with pain. I wrapped my arms around my boobs as I walked, to protect them.

The delicate subtlety of a cocked eyebrow and the shifty glance of my walking partner rapidly subsided.

"You're pregnant."

"You know, I think I might be."

"You are."

"I know."

"Honey, this is going to be *amazing*! I mean, this is the first time it's going to be real for you. Nineteen weeks in, my body has been undergoing serious changes and I can feel things happening. But for you, this undeniable vision of our child is going to blow your mind."

The preceding weeks had been ridiculously blissful. We couldn't believe our luck, pregnant first shot and my skin looked great. I liked it. We had signed up to our Consultant of Choice – well, my choice. Men don't have opinions on which obstetrician is best suited to your needs. Unless they are medical men, in which case, I'm sure they have more opinions than I would care to hear. At our first appointment we had been assured that, yes, I was pregnant and that everything looked perfectly normal.

Brilliant. No sickness, no aching, no back pain, nothing. Well, not quite nothing. During the first three months, I baked like Martha Stewart on speed. There was no fibre-rich carbohydrate that wasn't produced beyond possible consumption. Brown and white bread, muffins, tarts, pies, homemade muesli, biscuits, pancakes. I demonically pounded, kneaded and whisked until the fruits of my labour were being parcelled up and donated to builders, colleagues and small children. Then I hit the mystical crossroads of twelve weeks.

Twelve weeks means so much. Twelve weeks means: this is *real* now. Twelve weeks means: it's not your secret anymore.

That secret had been so precious to me. I had no desire to tell anyone. It was ours, our intimate, special thing. The minute it became common knowledge, it would not be ours anymore. Incredible sentiments for a big talker with a wide circle of friends with whom to share. Pregnancy does funny things to you.

The following seven weeks don't exist for me. I remember nothing. Just a blur of bump and clever wardrobe choices. But nineteen weeks; that, I remember.

Sitting in a Holles Street corridor outside a room marked "Scan", myself and Dave touch at many points along the lengths of our bodies, knees, hips, hands, shoulders. I play with my trusty digital camera to find the perfect setting to capture his look of childlike joy when he sees our baby on the monitor. I'm not even thinking of my own reaction. I'm in control.

"Now, hop up there, down to your bra and pants and we'll have a look. I'll pop a bit of this green paper over you in case anyone walks in."

"No. I'm grand, I'm not shy"

"Ah no, I'll stick it over you all the same."

"Okay."

"Now, let's have a look. This'll be a bit cold. Right, here we go."

Somehow I'm not holding the camera anymore.

"Right, now, there's both your babies lying beside each other now, lovely."

Mad, I muse, mad the way it looks like a mirror image, wonder why . . .

"What?"

"Both your babies . . . You knew you were having twins, right?"

Click. A photograph is taken. I look like I've been painted by Edvard Munch.

Thank you for the paper, nurse, I'll use it now to mop up the three litres of tears that are pouring from my eyes like a water feature. That's what I would have said, if I'd had the power of speech. Unfortunately I had not.

Dave dressed me and half-carried me towards the rooms of our Consultant of Choice. I think keening is the name for what I was doing.

We fell through the door like the wailing wall, heading for the receptionist. We wished to announce ourselves and apologise for our lateness, due to our unforeseen super-fertility. We were watched by a line of waiting mothers-to-be, twitching and startled like a small herd of springbok, though not as light on their feet. The receptionist politely suggested we wait outside. We weren't good for business in this condition.

Another corridor; I sat cocooned in an embrace, rocking and wailing. Uncontrollable tears that signified my first encounter with pure shock. Cartoon tears spurted out at a 90-degree angle to my head.

"Baby, are you okay? I have to go and put money in the meter or we'll get clamped. Honey, will you be okay? Just five minutes. Will you stay right here?"

He left me, rocking, wailing and nodding.

I needed to pee, I needed to ring Catherine.

I found a small toilet with two cubicles near my rocking spot. I found my phone and rang my lifeline.

"Catherine, it's twins."

Flatline.

"Catherine? CATHERINE! Are you there?"

"Oh Jesus. Oh Jesus. Oh Jesus. Where's Dave?"

"He's gone to put money in the meter."

"He may not come back."

I looked up during our conversation of tears and long pauses to find that, standing, I was being cradled in the bosom of an anonymous tall woman in her sixties, who rocked me, emitting comforting shushing sounds. I think I just smiled weakly at her, although I can't be sure.

"So, I know you think you're superwoman, but it's my duty, as your Consultant of Choice, to tell you that you're not. You have two babies in there and to mind them, you need to mind yourself. Your pregnancy, your babies and your own health are more important than work. If you work too long or too hard you will be putting yourself and your babies at significant risk. I'll see you in four weeks."

"Right."

This was not the plan. You see, I had a crèche organised from week one. A really good one. With a really long waiting list. I won't get two babies in there now.

I can't afford two babies in there.

I can't afford two babies.

"Baby, listen to me, I have to go back to work, will you be okay?"

"Don't leave me, don't ever leave me."

Numb shock and logistical disarray lasted for ten days. It was replaced by rising panic.

"So, this really is state-of-the-art in twin buggies. It's a back-and-front, three-wheel, titanium grey 'Jane' Powertwin. You won't do better. Not too heavy, not too light. It's a fabulous beast. Not cheap, but you won't need another vehicle."

Right.

Rollercoaster.com?

Right.

"We forgot to ask what we're having? I CAN'T BELIEVE WE FORGOT TO ASK!" I swerve into the hard shoulder and start to dial Holles Street.

"Sweetheart, are we sure we want to know?"

"OF COURSE WE BLOODY WANT TO KNOW! HAVEN'T WE HAD ENOUGH SURPRISES?"

"I'm sorry, I can't give out that information over the phone. Your Consultant of Choice suggests you wait until your next scan in three weeks' time."

Does she now?

I wake up with blurred vision, muddy-headed and confused. My babies – where are my babies? Caesarean scar notwithstanding, I hop out of bed and shuffle down a corridor towards the smell of newborn infant. I find Dave tenderly administering to our new family. He has 13 hours' experience on me and he looks like a pro.

"Aahh, this must be the mammy now. Well they're only gorgeous and the daddy's doing great work. Gentleman's family. Very common now, twins, aren't they?

Oh my God, I have two babies. Two more cartoon characters to add to the great graphic novel of my life.

Sonya Lennon is a stylist and co-presenter, along with Brendan Courtney, of RTÉ's Off the Rails.

If . . .

Fiona Looney

If I didn't have children, I would live in an apartment with a sea view instead of a boxy, semi-detached house in deepest suburbia. My local shop would be a delicatessen that sold four different types of sun-dried tomatoes instead of a Supervalu where you can collect stamps for weekend breaks you can never take.

I wouldn't have a dog, though I would reserve the right to borrow somebody else's for occasional long walks through verdant scenery while wearing Lainey Keogh jumpers. It goes without saying that this hired dog would never defecate.

I would be a Friend of the Theatre Festival, a patron of the Gate, an ally to the arts. I would be a first-night regular, and at the interval, I wouldn't eye up the champagne as though I'd never seen it before. I would never have been to see *The Tweenies Live* or *Bear in the Big Blue House* or *Disney On Ice*, and I would never, ever have purchased any sort of confectionery that comes in a bucket.

I would see all five movies on the Oscar Best Film shortlist every year instead of all the ones on the Best Animated Feature list. I would not be able to tell the difference between Disney and Pixar.

I would buy DVD box sets and, occasionally, I would even watch them. I would not know, in my heart of hearts, that I will not be able to watch all six seasons of *The Sopranos* – which completely passed me by – until I am retired. Sometimes I would watch DVDs in the afternoon and, if I felt like it, I might even have a glass of wine to enhance my viewing pleasure.

I would only wear a tracksuit for working out. And if I ever spotted some sick on it, I could at least take some consolation from the fact that it was my own.

I would go on holidays that I hadn't booked a year in advance. I would go on city breaks on a whim and I would have more than one stamp on my passport. I wouldn't look ten years older in my passport photo than I actually am.

I would eat out regularly and my passion for cooking wouldn't have got stuck somewhere in the mid-1990s. When the people who make *The Restaurant* asked me to do it, I wouldn't have had to cry off for fear of being found out. I wouldn't always know what's for dinner, days in advance. I could have lunch and stay out until well after tea-time. If I didn't produce three home-cooked meals a day, nobody would notice. I would never make a packed lunch that I wouldn't get to eat.

I wouldn't put money in envelopes for other people to go off and have a good time. I wouldn't need a cheque book. I wouldn't know how much piano lessons cost.

I might take piano lessons.

I would never have to read notes about nits and I wouldn't have one of those family planner calendars where everyone else's activity list was longer than my own, even though I was the busiest person on it.

"Working from home" would be a euphemism instead of a fact of life.

I would have written more plays and fewer sick notes. I would occasionally have sex without the covers on. I wouldn't have to keep my mobile phone on and I would never get texts about camogie fixtures.

I would have read every Booker short-listed novel of the past ten years and I would have at least attempted to have one of my own included on that noble list. I would read newspapers on the day they're published, instead of storing them up to read in bulk on long car journeys.

When I went to the gym, I could take a sauna. When that familiar knot of tension forms between my shoulder blades, I could have a massage instead of taking two paracetemol. I wouldn't get that knot of tension between my shoulder blades. I would still have long nails. I could take a bath instead of a shower and stay in it 'til my fingers wrinkled. I could use conditioner.

I could go to the shops without having to make a list. I could try on clothes in the actual shops instead of panic-buying everything and returning the majority of it afterwards. When I did buy something new and then tried it on at home, nobody in the room would snigger. I wouldn't need to use the washing machine every day.

I could go and see Shamrock Rovers more than a couple of times each season and I might even go to away games. I could go to the European Championships. When I go to

Dublin games, I could go to the pub afterwards instead of coming straight home with an exhausted boy. I could walk the pier without worrying that somebody would fall in.

I wouldn't have seen all my contemporaries promoted ahead of me. I wouldn't have to work at night. I would have fragile ornaments instead of Buzz Lightyear on my Habitat shelves. My body wouldn't force me out of bed at seven on a Saturday and Sunday morning. Nobody else's would either. I would never, ever have to drive. I wouldn't have life insurance. I wouldn't be in the VHI. If I died, it wouldn't ruin anyone else's life.

But if I lived in an apartment then I wouldn't have neighbours and I couldn't sit in my garden on those rare sunny summer evenings and hear the happy shrieks of kids playing on the road. And in the deli, I'd never get to hear about which local team had won or lost and who was pregnant and how much Amy's brace is going to cost. I would never discover how individuals become families, and how families become communities.

And if I spent my days writing books and plays and my nights at the theatre, then I'd never have learned to multi-skill and I wouldn't one day discover that I have somehow acquired a whole set of unexpected skills that make me a better, rounder person.

And if I ate out all the time, then I really would be a rounder person. And if I travelled a lot, then I'd have to spend more time in airports and I really, really hate airports. And my tracksuit is kind of comfortable.

And this morning, a little girl who's already a little too old for such things crawled into our bed for a cuddle and for the first time, I imagined weekends when we won't be woken by children and suddenly, those lie-ins didn't seem so precious. And later on, when her big sister went ice-skating with a bunch of other girls and a few boys – unsupervised for the very first time – I thought of Sunday afternoons that didn't involve waiting for an excited girl to arrive home and attempting to prise gossip out of her and they didn't seem quite so languid. And I had a Lainey Keogh jumper once and it would have been most unsuitable for walking the dog.

And there is a boy in the garden, pounding a ball into a goal and – any minute now – trailing mud and God knows what else all over the kitchen floor. And I will shout at him when he does and later on, he will talk knowledgeably with his Dad about Liverpool and check Dublin's National League fixtures with me. And when we spill out of Parnell Park together and onto the bus home, I know I won't miss the pub too much because we will need to discuss the new manager's tactics in great detail and in the pub, you can't hear yourself think.

It never stops. It is frantic. It is frustrating. It is occasionally heart-breaking. It is expensive. It is exhausting. It is exhilarating. It completes you, and sometimes it defeats you. It is like being on a rollercoaster that you can't stop, and all you can do is enjoy the ride, even when it throws your heart into your boots. Sometimes, my youngest will tell me she loves me "all the way to the library, all the way to planet Mars, three times round the moon and four times round the sun". She knows that I will always reply that I love her all that distance and back again. She is happy with that, but not nearly as happy as I am. That's what having kids does to you: it makes you happy. All the way to the library, all the way to planet Mars, three times round the moon, four times round the sun, and all the way back again.

And anyway, who really needs four types of sun-dried tomatoes?

Fiona Looney is a journalist, writer, broadcaster and mother of three – though not necessarily in that order. She is the author of two stage plays, Dandelions *and* October, *and a collection of her newspaper columns,* Misadventures in Motherhood. *She writes weekly columns in the* Irish Daily Mail *and the* Irish Mail on Sunday.

Child-proofing Your Home

Frank McNally

When moving into a new house, many people go to great lengths to ensure that the rooms are comfortable and pleasing to the eye. We consult home improvement magazines for advice on combining functionality with beauty. We may even hire an interior designer to ensure that the fitted kitchen goes well with the floor tiles and that the living room curtains are at least on speaking terms with the three-piece suite.

Then we have children, and suddenly we realise that our home is a terrible mistake. The children don't go with anything! Yes, they add splashes of colour here and there – but not in a good way. Worse, they clash violently – and all too often literally – with things: tables, bookshelves, walls. Everything except the ceilings, in fact.

We soon begin to question our sanity. What were we thinking when we bought that ridiculously expensive glass coffee table whose corners are perfectly positioned to poke a crawling infant's eyes out? And those glass doors that were designed to maximise the natural light! How long before our toddler crashes through them and maximises his head injuries?

You can't even blame the interior designer. If he'd been asked, which he wasn't, he would probably have advised you that children may be part of God's design, but as for interior design, they're against all the rules. You can have a beautiful home or a young family, but not both, he'd have told you. He'd probably have advised you to choose goldfish instead.

Nevertheless, here you are with a baby and a home that you now realise is a death trap. You have to make the best you can of the situation, and there are two basic choices: (1) you can house-proof the child, which would probably involve rearing it in a cage; or (2) you can try to child-proof the house. However great a challenge, most people opt for the latter.

Some things are just common sense. If you own any Ming vases, for example, now would be a good time to put them away somewhere safe (like Switzerland). The same goes for your Waterford Crystal collection, and the urn containing what's left of your grandfather. That priceless Persian rug in your living room at least has the advantage that it's not breakable. But unless you think its value would be enhanced by long-term exposure to baby emissions, yoghurt spills, saliva-covered half-eaten lollipops, etc., it will have to go too.

Let's assume you've already hidden away all the precious objects. The next step is to remove potential hazards from your child's path. The good news for paranoid parents is that this can be done over a period of time, as the infant's mobility grows. With a newborn baby, the number of accidents that can happen is fairly limited. I'd say it's in the low thousands, maximum. But for the purposes of this exercise, we'll include safety tips covering all the child's potential activities, from birth to ten years old.

Kitchen

The only things you really need to worry about here are the cooker, the kettle, the toaster, the washing machine, the dishwasher, the food-mixer, and anything else that ever contains hot water or electricity, or both. Also, all the presses containing any kind of material – shoe polish, Brillo pads, etc. – that will say to the average child: "Eat me!"

Pay particular attention to the microwave. The main risk here is that an infant may try to take something out while it's hot. But children are constantly mimicking their parents' behaviour. Left unsupervised, a child will experiment by placing inappropriate objects - the family pet, perhaps – into the microwave and then pressing "defrost".

Sharp objects should be kept out of reach. This is especially true when there's a new baby in the house and older siblings may be experiencing mixed feelings (in which case heavy, blunt objects should be kept out of reach as well).

The fridge is one of the safer items in your kitchen. But bear in mind that as your children grow older, they will spend increasing amounts of time standing in front of it with the door open and asking you if there's anything to eat. Hypothermia arising from exposure to open fridges is a big risk for teenagers in particular. Avoid choosing very low temperature settings, except in summer.

Living Room

Experts recommend that when child-proofing your house, you yourself should crawl around it on all fours to see what your pre-toddler will see. This can be an alarming experience, especially in the living room. You may notice for the first time that the lunatic who designed your house has placed all the plug sockets a foot off the floor! What was he thinking? Maybe he had shares in the company that makes those little plastic socket-fillers that you now have to buy before the baby electrocutes himself.

Other things that are about a foot off the floor are the aforementioned corners of the coffee table. There are no fewer than four of the damn things – all sharp enough to dent the forehead of a fast-moving toddler. Why on earth didn't you get a round table? Luckily, you can also buy little rubber table-corner attachments. Some of the better ones will stay in place for up to 48 hours before your child pulls them off and sticks them to the family pet instead.

If your living room has an open fireplace, it goes without saying that it will need a permanent guard from now on. Most parents can't afford to pay a permanent guard's wages, however. You'll probably have to make do with a part-time one, or just put one of those metal grids around the fireplace instead.

Another big risk is the bookshelf, which your child will mistake for a climbing frame. Free-standing bookshelves and free-standing toddlers don't mix. Even where the bookshelf is fixed to the wall, make sure that the heavier volumes are on the lower shelves. You don't want his first encounter with the *Complete Works of Shakespeare* to prejudice him for life against Elizabethan drama.

Other things to be aware of are wires. In common with rodents, teething children will chew on these if let. Cover them up or put them in protective tubes (the wires, that is, not the children). And finally: be careful you don't put too many toys in the playpen. Like a prisoner of war, your child will consider it his first duty to escape. Tunnelling may not be an option, but toys can be piled up against the perimeter fence and climbed, with disastrous results.

Bathroom
At the risk of overdoing it, you might want to put a child lock on the toilet seat. Otherwise children will place inappropriate objects – e.g., the family pet – down the bowl. They may also put themselves down the bowl, of course. But even if this were not a risk, there are always extra hygiene issues when you have small children in the house. A toilet-lid lock can be a big comfort to a parent on those occasions when he notices that his toothbrush is wet even before he uses it.

By contrast, you should remove any key or other locking device from the bathroom door, or else your child will manage to lock itself in eventually. Trying to talk a child through unlocking a door from the other side is like being a member of air traffic control staff and advising a nervous passenger how to land a plane.

On the face of it, not having a lock on the bathroom door exposes you to invasion of privacy. But remember, you're a parent now. Your privacy was invaded, by land and air, the day your first child was born. It's now permanently occupied and the remaining few pockets of resistance will be wiped out soon. Nobody's coming to liberate it, either.

Bedroom

While your child's bed may serve as a place for him to sleep (on the rare occasions when he's not sleeping in yours), its main function is of course as a trampoline. Occasionally, he will fall off the trampoline, and you need to take this into account. Assuming a particularly bad bounce, you should calculate the distance from his bed that your child can travel and then remove all dangerous objects, including windows, from within that radius.

Dressing tables will inevitably be used as launching pads for jumping onto the bed. Depending on your preference, you should move them (a) far enough away from the bed to prevent jumping or (b) close enough to reduce the risk of the jumper missing the target.

As well as being a place of physical safety, the bedroom should be a haven of calm and reassurance. When your child is three or four years old, you may need to check his room last thing at night for monsters. Under the bed is the key area here.

A Few General Points

It goes without saying that you need safety gates at the top and bottom of your stairs. Ideally, all windows at child height should be either double-glazed or bricked up – whichever you consider safer. Cat flaps are a particular risk for toddlers. Fire is a constant danger, so hide matches and cigarette lighters. If your child has a scientific bent, you should also hide magnifying glasses, sticks that can be rubbed together, etc.

Even if you remove all obvious furniture hazards from your house, children still risk collision with walls. If you have a particularly athletic child, you might want to fit him with a crash helmet – just for the first few years. And finally, if you have one or more male children, a useful tip is to smash all your good furniture now; it will save time later on.

The main thing is to keep things in perspective. It's impossible to eliminate all potential dangers. Even if you fitted the house with every child-proofing device on the market, you'd still need eyes in the back of your head – an option that, despite all the advances in science, is still not available at time of going to press. The good news is that, as a parent, you will develop a sixth sense (or "become neurotic", to give it its scientific term) about possible danger, and you can usually rely on this to alert you.

Even then, if you considered all the potential hazards your home poses to your child (and vice versa), you'd probably abandon the house and move the family into a large tent in the back garden until the kids were reared. After all, tents are soft, have no glass windows, rarely consist of more than one floor, and what's more are one hundred per cent wipeable. And you know what? That's not such a bad idea.

Frank McNally is chief writer of "An Irishman's Diary" in The Irish Times. *He lives in Dublin with his wife and three children.*

Conception

Sean Moncrieff

No one ever writes about conception. Pick up any of the huge range of *Nervous Parent* books and there will be lots about giving birth in a bath while dolphins circle around; but nothing about how you, the parent, actually got there.

And how you got there usually starts with a conversation; a conversation which the man, I suspect, never sees coming. Of course, in the age of the weepy in-touch-with-his-feelings man, many of them will claim that it wasn't a surprise at all; that he and his partner had a meeting of minds and body clocks and, in a caring and nurturing environment – while a school of dolphins serenaded them with pan pipes – they decided to make a baby.

We were living in London when we had our little chat. In London and having a nice time, thank you very much. We were the Ryanair generation, able to skip home for the weekend if the mood took us or the finances allowed. We were confident, educated, middle-class and finally free of any maudlin attachment to the home country. Back then, Ireland was starting to be regarded as a bit cool; thus we, as its young representatives, were a bit cool also.

But cool is slightly more tricky to maintain when you hit the grand old age of thirty. I dealt with this traumatic event by trying to ignore it as much as possible and by deciding to give up cigarettes, my logic being that this would help me maintain my youthful looks. It wasn't easy, of course: for weeks I endured vivid and terrifying nightmares while during the day I would find myself staring wistfully into the windows of tobacconists, fighting the urge to buy fancy lighters I would never use.

Sleep-deprived and with my body tormented by the lack of nicotine, I never noticed that my wife was dealing with her Significant Birthday in a completely different way. For her, the start of the Third Decade also launched the incessant ticking of her body clock – a din apparently so loud she thought I could hear it also.

Thus, she assumed I wouldn't be surprised when she almost casually mentioned that it was time we had a baby. It was on a Saturday afternoon, and included in a list of other things we had to do: the laundry, visit Sainsburys, have a baby.

Stifling a yawn and pretending to smoke a pencil, I quickly realised that there were few objections I could raise. Nature was putting the pressure on; we could either agree to start the conception process now or face a lifetime of regret and recrimination. We would witness the slow withering of my wife's womb, and all because I didn't want to grow up.

"Okay," I said weakly. "Okay."

Of course, I only said it because I didn't quite believe it would happen. The whole process seemed too remote and fantastic to have anything to do with us. And anyway, I was immediately distracted by what my wife said next.

"So you'll have to learn to drive, yes?"

This was something else I had been meaning to do, but at the time there was no great need as Bridget did all the driving, and liked it that way. In principle, I had no objection to learning, though to ask me to get behind the wheel of a car when I was hysterical with sleep- and nicotine-deprivation seemed a crazy idea. I was quick to point this out, only to realise that I had already been outmanoeuvred.

"Sean, you can't expect me to drive when I'm nine months' pregnant. You'll have to drive me to the hospital. There's a baby to think about now."

In the space of a five-minute conversation, my life had changed utterly.

Not that I realised it at the time; at the time I still clung to the possibility that this was a notion which would go off her; and anyway, the whole plan was contingent upon some mysterious process over which we had no control.

Afterwards, we counted it back. We had the conversation on a Saturday. We reckon she was pregnant by the following Tuesday.

I don't wish to brag, but my wife and I are Olympic-standard breeders: every time we wanted one, we were able to produce a pregnancy in jig time; and once or twice when we didn't want to.

Because we'd seen it on some film, we bought three different pregnancy test kits. All came up positive. Bridget burst into tears, took to the bed and wouldn't talk to me for three hours. I sat in the kitchen, drinking tea, dying for a cigarette and enjoying the strange macho glow of knowing that I'd hit the back of the net first time.

The first person I told was my driving instructor. In some strange way, I felt I owed him this: he, probably without realising it, had been the one person most instrumental in preparing me for the grown-up world of parenthood. Tony had a very distinct driving lesson style: short on actual driving and long on talking about driving. The first day we met, I drove a total of twenty yards and spent the rest of the hour listening to Tony tell me that I was a natural; that he had been teaching for years and knew simply from my posture that I would pass my test first time. I could have walked away from a blazing car wreck – with Tony still inside – and still felt good about my motoring abilities.

As the weeks went on the driving-talking ratio in the lessons did swing back in favour of driving, yet every lesson would end with at least fifteen minutes of chat, during which time I would again be told what a superbly talented wheelman I was. But we would range onto other subjects also. Tony would talk openly about his three failed marriages, about his current relationship with a nurse. One day – while I was still driving – he cheerfully informed me that despite all her years of medical experience, the girlfriend nurse had told Tony the instructor that his was the largest penis she had ever seen.

It was at this point that I began to wonder if I should get myself a new instructor – a notion which Bridget began promoting quite vehemently as time went on. At first, when she still had a neat bump, when we still marvelled at the undulations in her stomach every time the baby moved, it was all a bit of a joke: "Sean's new Best Friend" or even "Sean's Boyfriend". But by the time we hit the last three months, when the baby kicking was waking us both up at night and Bridget began to think of herself as a beached whale, the humour of the situation had all but evaporated.

"When are you going to do the test?"

This was the oft-repeated question. Bridget would say it to me and I would relay it to Tony, who would then make me park up and give a twenty-five minute answer, most of which I would have forgotten by the time I got home.

As far as Tony was concerned, I wasn't quite ready, yet Bridget and I began to suspect that he might have other motives: he was dragging out the lessons for the money or, even more weirdly, for the company.

And time was running out.

So, being a man, I of course confronted the issue head-on. I made some excuse to Tony, cancelled a lesson and took a session with someone else. I felt like an adulterous swine. He was a nice enough chap, small and polite, but there was virtually no talk. Just driving. Lots of driving. At the end I asked him if he thought I was ready to take my test.

He shrugged.

In that one gesture, Tony's months of careful ego-building came crashing down. Now I wasn't sure if I had learned anything from the man. But there was no option: I had to book my test. I tried practice drives with my wife in the car, but that nearly ended in divorce, and on one particularly bad trip, a murder-suicide. I had one more lesson with Mister

Shrug and didn't respond to the message Tony left on the answering machine. I told myself he was probably used to this sort of thing.

Yet, somewhat miraculously, I did hear from Tony again. About three weeks later he left another message, this time an apology for cancelling a lesson two days previously. Perhaps he had mixed me up with someone else, or phoned my number by accident – or perhaps it was an awkward ploy to re-establish contact. I didn't give it much thought. I rang Tony straight back to tell him the fantastic news that I had indeed passed my test on the first go, just as he had predicted; that now I could be a proper father and drive my wife to the hospital.

"Oh," said Tony in a puzzled tone of voice. "Okay. What's your name again?"

I silently vowed never to trust a driving instructor ever again.

But, on the other hand, there was plenty to be positive about. I had passed my test, the cigarette cravings had abated considerably and finally – *finally* – the arrival of the baby was but days away. Not that we could quite believe this: the final trimester seemed to drag along so slowly that at times we believed that Bridget would always be pregnant, doomed to drag her bulging belly around the world forever, to have to say to people: "He just didn't want to come out. So we left him there." Even when the contractions started – conveniently, at four in the morning – Bridget woke me up to say she was having period pains.

So at last, I got to drive her to the hospital. Perhaps my wife had suggested that I learn to drive out of sheer practicality, or perhaps, due to some spooky prescience on her part, she realised that it might be a good idea to give me at least one useful thing to do that day.

It's of course all right and proper that the partner be there on the day of the birth, but have no illusions: when the pain really starts to kick in, the man is functionally useless. All he can do is coo encouraging phrases, not take the abuse personally and not let on that he wants to gag at the sight of all that blood.

Some time that afternoon I staggered out of the Royal Free Hospital in Hampstead, trying to remember where I parked the car and how to get into first gear and wondering if I were to have a cigarette now – just one – would that constitute going back on them?

The next few days were equally blurry: driving back and forth to the hospital, making and taking phone calls and discovering that I could walk into a chemist's and ask for sanitary towels without a trace of embarrassment. And then they left the hospital and came home with me – though I must admit that at the time it didn't feel like a *them*; it felt like Bridget, but now with different work to do. The baby was still *the baby*, somehow an extension of her rather than anything I had a part in making.

One of the best parenting decisions we ever made was to divide up the sleeplessness. The night was halved into shifts: I would cover midnight to 4.00 a.m.; Bridget would cover 4.00 a.m. to 8.00 a.m. This system worked exceptionally well, except for the odd occasion when our new son might sleep through until 4.01 – a situation which would prompt the hasty re-opening of negotiations. But on most nights he would wake when he was supposed to and let out a little gurgle, and I would stagger out of bed, scoop him up and with only one eye open heat a bottle, plonk in front of the television (mostly '70s cop shows or a truly atrocious music programme called *The Hit Man and Her*), feed him, burp him, change him and have him back in bed within half an hour.

And it was on one of these nights, with Pete Waterman on the TV mouthing inanities about some long-forgotten band, that I looked down at my little son gurgling on his bottle and realised how hopelessly I loved him; that the constant sleeplessness and the smell of puke were things of dizzy joy.

This realisation hit me with the force of a truck: held me on the sofa until dawn began to peek over the trees. And from then on I felt different – bigger, somehow, as if my soul had expanded to take in more than my own selfish concerns.

The ability to drive hadn't made me a man; this had.

He's seventeen now and promises he would puke again (and not in a wondrous way) if I ever say such things to his face. We called him Sencha, which we found in a book of Irish fairy stories edited by W.B. Yeats and Lady Gregory. Sometimes he asks why we gave him such a weird name. We say: "Well, it was that, or Tony . . ."

Sean Moncrieff is the author of four books, the father of four children and the host of Moncrieff *every weekday afternoon on Newstalk 106–8.*

The Imperfect Mother

Sinead Moriarty

As I get older and my friends and contemporaries take on more responsibility in their jobs and lives, the one thing I realise is that everyone is winging it. This discovery is as frightening as it is reassuring. When we are young, we think our parents know everything. Now, as a parent to two young boys, I realise that my parents, like me, knew nothing. They were, as I am now, winging it.

With motherhood comes the realisation that you haven't got a clue what you're supposed to do. How can I, who is still working out who I am, teach two small boys who they are? How can I make these sweet little people into strong, independent, kind, compassionate, well-rounded individuals? How can I ensure that I don't mess it up?

Answer = you can't. You can only learn from your mistakes. There are no guarantees. There is no right or wrong way. There is only the advice my mother used to give me going into exams: "Just do your best; that's all anyone can ask."

The difference between the experience of baby number one and baby number two is simply this – you stop kidding yourself that you're ever going to be the perfect parent and realise that getting through the day without broken furniture, broken bones and broken sleep is a miracle in itself.

Coming Home

When your first child is born, you gaze into their little red face and promise to cherish and nurture them forever. You take them home to their beautifully decorated nursery and lay them down in freshly laundered sheets and play them Mozart on the specially designed cot mobile that you ordered from the *"my baby's going to be a world leader.com"* website.

When your second child is born, you stagger home, put them in the hall in their car seat and lavish the first child with gifts and attention in case they feel left out or usurped and have one of their epic tantrums. In the meantime, you forget entirely about the new baby until they roar for food.

Getting the Baby into a Routine

Routine is what all new mothers become obsessed with. We all want a baby that sleeps through the night. Suddenly, you find yourself in competition with other new Mums over sleep patterns. Everyone rushes out to buy baby books that promise to have your child in a routine within weeks of its birth. These books cause women the world over to have nervous breakdowns trying to force their children into draconian regimes that, looking back now, I can see as absolutely ludicrous. . . . Ah the wisdom of hindsight! And yet, as a brand new mother, I duly went out and bought these "bibles" for babies. I studied them with intense concentration and a highlighter pen. According to the authors, my child would be sleeping thought the night within six weeks. I tried to follow these ridiculous routines and almost went out of my mind. Eventually I realised that the person I had to listen to was my baby and not a bunch of "*über*-nannies" who seemed to believe that children were robots.

When my second child arrived, I fed him when he roared, I changed his nappy when it needed changing and I let him sleep when he was tired. Life was a lot simpler.

Weaning

When your first child is being weaned from milk to solids, you buy cook books by glossy-haired American women with big teeth called Annabelle. You study the recipes with the concentration of a rocket scientist, highlighting all the most nutritious ones. Suddenly, leeks, celery and lentils become part of your shopping list. You stay up until all hours, steaming, simmering and pureeing foods that you have never cooked before in your life. You are determined that your baby will have baby purees that provide them with a good source of protein, beta-carotene, folate (no I have no idea what that is either!), fibre and vitamin C.

Every time baby number two opens its mouth, you shove whatever is closest to hand into it – this can involve chocolate biscuits, crisps, crusts of bread, sugar cubes, car keys, pens or whatever else happens to be lying around.

Soothers

When your first child is born you refuse to put a soother into their mouth. God forbid! They give the children bucked teeth and distort their speech patterns. There is no way your precious child is going to be nicknamed Bugs Bunny in school. Listening to them wailing is just part of being a parent.

Before your second child takes its first breath you shove a soother into its mouth. There is barely room for them in the cot, because you have filled it with fifteen soothers in the futile hope that every time they roll over, one will pop voluntarily into their mouth and save you having to get up at night and re-plug them.

Discipline

When your first child begins to have toddler tantrums, you worry yourself sick. Why? What did I do wrong? Are they sick? In pain? Did I get the words of "Incy Wincy Spider" wrong? You try to talk to them as they continue to scream into your face. When they throw themselves on the floor of the supermarket because you put raspberry yogurts into the trolley instead of strawberry ones, you go straight home and spend all night researching anger management on the internet. When they fling a plate of food at you because you can't find their favourite red spoon, you book an appointment with a neurologist because you think they might be bi-polar.

When your second child thrown their first tantrum, you laugh. When they throw their second, you put them in their cot and leave them there until they calm down . . . settling down outside their bedroom with a good book, as you now know that this could take from two minutes to two hours.

First Day at School

When your eldest is going to school, you buy them a new outfit for the special day. You get up an hour early to make them a nutritious breakfast and to get yourself ready for the big day, changing ten times as you desperately try to get the "casual but stylish Mum" outfit right. You take fifty photos of them before they leave the house. You try not to cry the whole way there and you bawl the whole way home. You collect them early and bombard the teacher with questions and cannot believe that she hasn't noticed that they are a particularly gifted child and definitely a future world leader.

When your second child goes to school, they wear their sibling's hand-me-down outfit. You forget to charge the camera so no pictures can be taken. You throw a raincoat over your pyjamas and try to suppress the feeling of glee as you leave them in and look forward to the first morning you've had to yourself in four years. When you pick them up you pray that the teacher won't tell you they've bitten or thumped anyone.

The School Gate (AKA The War Zone)

When your first child is an hour old, you fill in the application forms for the top five schools in your area. You know they'll probably win a scholarship when the time comes, but just in case, you don't want be without a back up plan. Other mothers assure you that you will have to sell your soul to the devil to get your child into a good school. They warn you that *nobody* can get into certain schools without serious contacts or the financial ability to build a new library, gymnasium or running track.

On your second child you realise that this is twaddle and that as long as they are able to walk and talk they have a good chance of getting into one of the schools in your neighbourhood and that it really doesn't matter which one.

Play Dates

Your first child's play date can be traumatic. You don't really know this woman or her child. Will they be kind to your first-born? Will they clap and cheer when your little genius builds a Lego tower like you do? Do they have dangerous toys in the house? Will they allow the children to play outside with no coats on? What kind of snack will the mother give them? Will they, God forbid, allow them to watch television?!!

If anyone is kind enough to ask your second child on a play date, you're giddy with joy. Two hours of calm in your house is such a rare treat. You don't care if they watch TV, eat sweets or play outside naked.

Birthday Parties

When it comes to your eldest child's third birthday, you go all out. You start baking weeks in advance. You do a crash course in cake-making and spend days creating a dragon cake that even the mothers "ooh" and "aah". You decorate the house from top to toe. You invite everyone in the class. Twenty-six screaming children will be no problem; you want your child to be popular and well-liked. It takes three days to clean up and the red icing you used for the dragon cake never comes out of your cream carpet, curtains or sofas.

When it comes to your second child's third birthday, you invite the five friends they mention the most to the local indoor play jungle. You valiantly ignore the smell of urine that permeates the place and try to look positively on the burnt chicken nuggets and soggy chips that make up the birthday dinner. A football cake from Tescos is produced and once the singing is over you go home to a clean house, flop on the couch, put your feet up and sink a bottle of wine.

Why?

When your first-born begins to question things, you're thrilled. All gifted children want to understand the ways of the world. You answer every question diligently and if, God forbid, you don't know the answer because dinosaurs are not your forte, you immediately look it up and provide a detailed response in record time. I found myself constantly calling my nephews to quiz them on why exactly Spiderman would outfight Batman, Hulk, Shadow and the Silver Surfer in a fight?

On your second child, you feign deafness or just pure ignorance because you know their thirst for knowledge is insatiable. It's eight o'clock at night, you have no more energy left and frankly you couldn't give a toss if Spiderman got his head kicked in by all his enemies and his arms ripped off and eaten by an enormous T-Rex.

From Cot to Bed

When your first child is two, you decide it's time they slept in their own bed. Besides, you need the cot for the new baby. You go out and buy the nicest bed you can find with an extortionately priced "super-safe" mattress and beautiful bed-linen. When your eldest child comes home, screams all night and refuses point blank to ever sleep in that nasty bed, you go out and buy a second cot.

When your second child is thirteen, you agree to get them a bed.

And so, at this early stage in my experience of parenting, I struggle every day to be the best I can be – some days I go to bed happy with myself; most days I go to bed worrying that I have said or done something that will damage them for life. In my experience, parenthood comes packaged with a lifetime of worry and self-flagellation.

So, what's the upside? An unconditional love and pride that leaves you breathless every time you look at them . . .

Sinead Moriarty has had five books published to date. With her third child recently born, the sixth may take longer than anticipated to complete!

Get on the Bus

Pól Ó Conghaile

I hadn't expected a bus to drive right through our living room.

There it was, however – honking along on a cold October evening, clanging the bell as if for the first time. "Get in the back, beside Baby Amy and George the Monkey," a very bossy driver demanded. "And don't move Pogo."

Ay, caramba! One day, I was propping up a baby. The next, my two-and-a-half-year-old daughter is driving a couch loaded with stuffed animals. She clangs that bell again – an antique, the use of which causes her mother's eyebrow of admonishment to levitate – and off we go. Next stop? The farm/armchair. ET has some animal noises to make, and we're already running late.

One day a baby. The next a blustering bus driver. Where has the time gone?

Before Rosa arrived, I travelled to insecure countries. My life was uninsured. If I was tired, I slept. Now, everything is wrung through the parental calculus. I travel less, and for shorter periods. I go to my GP for check-ups. I own life assurance. I have gained an inconceivably beautiful angle on living, sure. But I have lost the pleasure of going to the bathroom alone, staying up past 11pm on a weeknight, of Mum and Dad leaving the house together without a babysitting meter running at €10 an hour.

I used to kid myself, too, that I had never lost my capacity for wonder. Rosa dashed that on the head in one fell swoop. I look at chalk and see chalk. She sees an instrument for making magical circles you're not allowed to step outside of without shouting "Pingo!" I look at a jug and see a jug. She sees a bath for her animals to clean themselves up before bedtime.

In a recent interview, I asked author and filmmaker Rebecca Miller about her experiences of parenthood. "Once you have a child, I really do believe that you cross this river," she said. "Before you have a child, all of these people on the other side are waving and you think you know what they look and feel like – i.e. a) you're boring, and b) you can't finish a sentence because your kids interrupt you. But then you go across the river, and you understand."

Becoming a mother, Miller said, gave her "a new sense of empathy for the exhaustion and fears that you have; the kind of mistakes that you make, that you might make, and that you're afraid of making . . . my children have already forgotten half the things that I treasure so deeply . . . they're trying to become individuals, throw you off in a way and then you're left, like the lover who has been abandoned! And that's life! That's the way it is!"

The word "lover" feels wrong, but it feels right too. Rosa grins and my heart gulps. When she arrived, it felt like I had finally gotten to the bottom of something. Then came this comet of a kid, and I realised I hadn't gotten to the bottom of anything. The bottom was false. And beneath it was a bottomless pit. Somewhere, as I write, I'm in freefall.

Miller was also unafraid to talk about the darker side of parenthood. The sinister fuses that crackle and fizz when you've been rocking a colicky baby for hours; the despair you feel when you can't go to the toilet alone; the hysterical weeping as you fumble for Calpol at 3.00 a.m., looking and feeling like something from *Dawn of the Dead*. In one of her books, she likens a claustrophobic mother/daughter relationship to having a plastic bag over one's head. In another episode, a mother dreams that her children are eating her ribs. Her reaction? To offer them barbeque sauce.

Childrearing is easy compared with, say, mining diamonds or managing Sunderland, but it definitely has its moments. Recently, for instance, my little girl had her first nightmare. In the middle of the night, a scream cut through the walls – hauling me out of the bed like a fish on a line. I rushed in to find her bolt upright, wide-eyed, convinced that a witch had been pulling at her sheets. That was hard. Hugging my girl as, heart thumping, she grasped for some understanding of what she'd seen, made me afraid too. Coaxing her back to sleep, I never felt more strongly the fact that, although I was 32 years older, four foot taller and ten stone heavier, I could do nothing to stop that nightmare coming again. That night, or any night.

As a parent, your instinct is to take on any pain coming your kids' way, to protect them from any danger you can. I can lift Rosa up when a dog barks or hold her hand in traffic, but I know that when she's a big girl, I won't be able to protect her from anything much at all. That's hard too. But to see my child grow certain again because I was there to whisper her down from her nightmare – well, that's bloody beautiful.

"Treasure it" is the single most common piece of advice I get from empty-nesters. "It goes by so fast."

Time moves at two speeds in our house. If toddler is tetchy, the clock moves at a crawl. Sometimes, it's all we can do to focus on 8.00 p.m., pull on our lazy pants and crash onto the couch (we watched all 60 episodes of *The Wire* in a matter of weeks). Simultaneously, the years brush by in a blur. I take a photo album off the shelf and the little girl in the pictures seems so small, so baby-like. Her hair is short, her face barely emerging from its chubbiness. Hang on a second. Where did she go?

It's true too that this is a unique time to be a Dad. Irish parents are getting older, families smaller and far more women are working. "The lines between genders are blurring," as Matt O'Connor of Fathers 4 Justice told me in another interview. Fathers roles are evolving – but into what?

I guess we're more David Coleman than Dr Spock. We're not embarrassed to wear slings, we change nappies and we realise that fatherhood involves more than disciplining children and asking them to fetch your slippers. On the other hand, many of us not having experienced emotionally involved fathering whilst growing up ourselves, modern Dads run the risk of failure where previous generations were never expected to succeed.

I think society is getting to grips with this, however. We've grown wise to the fact that twenty-first-century parents can't all be like David Beckham or Miriam

O'Callaghan. We've realised that, amazing though the rewards may be, burning the candle at both ends comes with a price – zombie-like exhaustion, bad backs and a toddler's tolerance for alcohol.

Trouble is, Irish institutions have yet to fully catch up with Irish parents. There's no provision in employment law for paternity leave, for example. Dads looking to take time off for sick kids or family days are regarded as exotic girly-men, and women wishing to pursue a career are expected to do so without sacrificing so much as a minute of motherhood.

"It's not worth it," says one friend, regarding his job. Lately, he's been eating into overtime, regularly leaving the house before his son wakes and getting home after he has gone to bed. "Three days without seeing your kid . . . that's f—ked up."

And that's not even getting started on traffic, childcare or the price of Clark's shoes.

For me, parenting can be all-consuming – sometimes dangerously so. I am hyper-conscious of how formative my own childhood memories seem, how larger-than-life they are, of the fact that Rosa's are coming and going as I speak and write. Life is happening as we make plans. I want every day to be new, but at the same time I don't want to force my own preoccupations on someone who clearly has just as good a time tearing sheets out of a notebook as visiting an aquarium or going on an adventure walk.

In fact, some of our best memories are of staying in. The day we made The Incredible House™ out of a cardboard box. The time we made doctors' outfits and diagnosed all manner of illnesses in those adaptable teddies. We once made a painting out of crushed leaves; I remember the first time Rosa tasted jelly; and I treasure the fleeting moments when she slows down for a second, lies beside me on the bed, and has her gossipy chats.

As a Dad, I've been granted a whole new set of fears. A sore throat is never a sore throat anymore – it is always the symptom of a tumour, or angina. When older parents talk about teenage boys, I want to become the owner of a shotgun. I'm conscious that everyone on the Irish rugby team is younger than I am. Age is relative, of course (my wife completely opposes me on this – she embraces growing older; I hate it), and to Rosa, I am the strongest, handsomest, most reliable man on earth. But inside, more than anything, I fear dying or not being able to provide for my little girl.

No matter how wintry these thoughts get, however, every morning a little shrub pushes through the stony soil and blooms afresh. My girl stirs from her bed. She hits the house with such energy, such absence of cynicism or resignation that I can't but be borne along. She wheels a doll in a buggy as if it is saving lives. She eats her cereal as if for the first time. She gets as engrossed in her toy basket as Joyce did in *Finnegans Wake*. And I fall in love all over again.

Am I any the wiser? The one thing people love more than coo-cooing at newborn babies is coo-cooing at newborn babies whilst telling you they don't come with a manual. This is true. Before I became a Dad, I read the kind of books that get reviewed in newspapers. Now, my bedside pile includes Penelope Leech (the Delia Smith of child-rearing) and the aforementioned David Coleman. A recent report by Foresight, the UK government's futures think tank, likened the adolescent brain to a car with a strong engine but poor steering. The toddler's brain is more like an X-wing fighter piloted by a monkey on crack – with one of those in the house, you need support literature.

As I write, for example, we are dealing with a catchphrase: "I don't want to." It's our household's version of Pierre, the boy who would only say, "I don't care." Time for bed? "I don't want to." Time for dinner? "I don't want to." Time for a visit to Junglemania with all of your friends? "I don't want to." It's like a 16-year-old is trapped in a two-year-old's body.

As for advice, I advocate taking it rather than giving it. However, there are a couple of things that have worked so overwhelmingly well or badly in our lives that I feel justified in passing them on.

Control food before food controls you. Even if this is the only thing you do right from the ages of 0 to 18, you will have earned your stripes as a parent. "There is no child on earth who will eat a vegetable, once they've seen a biscuit," as Andrew Clover, author of *Dad Rules* (another bedside pile staple) puts it.

Don't do TV. I realise I am issuing this advice as a father-of-one, and will likely in later years use the box as a babysitter. But for now, my take is that TV should be at most a ten- or fifteen-minute gear-change before bedtime. If it's always on, that's what kids expect. If it's always off, they'll expect that too. What's there to lose? Are any of us going to die wishing we'd watched more TV?

Let the child come to you. Sit back. Appear cool and disinterested. Do not bound about like a Billy-goat because you've decided they need some quality time. Watch what happens – by doing nothing in this way, it is quite possible to commit an act of parenthood (N.B. this is not a licence to start reading the newspaper).

Dressing a small child is like trying to give a cat a bath. The trick lies in reading her movements and learning to intercept them with a) sleeves or b) trouser legs. Once you master the art of pre-emptive dressing, things get positively Zen.

If you're in the mood for laughs, do a running commentary on whatever your kid is doing. There's something subtle at play here – you're validating their actions, or some such twaddle – but more importantly it makes everybody feel giddy. "Oh, I see. You're watering the books so they can grow into big trees that everybody can read from far away. And you're wearing a Happy Hat too. What a great idea!" Think of yourself as the George Hamilton of child-rearing. Your kid will love this. Not so much if they're a teenager, mind.

And that completes the thoughts of this over-tired, money-haemorrhaging, love-bedraggled man who was never happier than the day his daughter pointed at him and said: "That's my Daddy."

Pól Ó Conghaile is a journalist and author of That's My Baby! *(Poolbeg).*

We've Come a Long Way, Baby

Áine O'Connor

In June 1995 I was in Mexico, in a place called Puerto Escondido. It was an early to bed, early to rise, all the better to catch the waves surfers' paradise where smoking tobacco was frowned upon as unhealthy but smoking grass was okay. There were surfers and surfer chicks from all over the world – American, Australian, South African, French, Brazilian. And my friend and I. Neither of whom could balance on a stationary surf board on a beach, much less on a wave hurtling towards shore. No matter; we had breakfast with them when they came off the Pacific, paddled enthusiastically and learned interesting facts about geography, surfing and ice cream headaches.

It was a fairly wild trip. And proof that, although at times life feels like it stands still, years running into one another in an ever-increasing rush of mushed time, sometimes it doesn't take that long for everything to change.

In June 1996 I was a maternity hospital, screaming, in between incomprehensible animal howls, that this was "not natural". (I still agree with myself – the logistics are WRONG.) I was in labour, waiting for the emergence of my first child.

I come from a long line of eldest daughters and had been convinced that this, my first child, would be fulfilling her family destiny, another spoke in the eldest daughter wheel, a fact I'd merely sought to have confirmed at the twenty-week scan. "Oh there's the little willy." Willy? What's my daughter doing with a willy? Baffled but no less delighted, I spent the walk back to work ringing people on my new-fangled mobile phone to revise earlier predictions and tell them I'd be having a boy.

I'd read up on everything, done my birth plan, hired a TENS machine. All of which I had flung aside as useless within approximately twenty minutes of contractions starting. After a brief attempt at stoicism I went for the screaming and begging for drugs option because nothing quite prepares you for the pain of labour and delivery, for the pain and sheer agricultural spectacular that is the entire process. Nowhere is sacred, nowhere. I remain utterly baffled by anyone who says birth is beautiful.

In my defence, it was a difficult birth. More than 24 hours after the contractions began, I was lying on a delivery table and it seemed that the only person who hadn't showed up, and wasn't planning to any time soon, was the star of the show – my son. Two midwives had become four, then appeared a doctor, another and a paediatrician. I was aware that this wasn't good, but in an abstract way because I had taken refuge in the gas mask and one of the midwives seemed to be now fully employed trying to get me to ease up on the Entonox. Even though I felt it was only a matter of time before she put her sensibly shod foot on my face in an attempt at greater leverage, there was no chance I was releasing my grip on the only thing there I could control – those precious numbing vapours.

The pregnancy had been a surprise. But the biggest surprise for me, 27, devotedly liberated, vocal eschewer of all things traditionally female, was quite how pleased I was to be pregnant. Circumstances were less than ideal but it, he, had made his presence felt from so early on. I thought of him as my little Alpha foetus. He'd defied a morning-after pill, a fall down some Aztec steps, bleeding, a clinic, logic maybe. I'd had violent morning, noon and night sickness until 16 weeks. He gave thunderous belly-shuddering kicks from 20 weeks. My bump was undeniable, unmistakable; he was just so there. Although I knew great kindness and support from people, I have never felt so utterly lonely. To me that pregnancy was he and I in a permanent cuddle, he and I against the world, the beginnings of a love I'd never felt before.

I'd been too superstitious to buy anything at all, no clothes, no buggy, no supplies. Nothing until the month before the baby was due and even then I'd bought only the hospital required minimum: babygros, vests, nappies and that classic first-time mother mistake – something neat with wings instead of those industrial-strength maternity pads they sell in Mothercare, a mistake that involves partners, friends and/or mothers running straight back to Mothercare after a day of failure with wings.

The only exception to the superstitious plan ban was an early one, about 14 weeks in, when hardly anyone knew and there was no outward sign: two newborn babygros in the Next sale. They were £2.50 each. They were tiny. They were stripy. They were unisex. They were an act of faith, or hope. And I'd take them out like talismans whenever things felt difficult.

Towards the end of the pregnancy, I really just wanted to meet this little man. I knew him, I loved him, I just wanted to see him. It felt like a formality, so I was really excited when I'd woken with pains at 6.00 a.m. on 17 June. A day early. But here on the delivery table, the sun streaming through the windows in the very early morning of the following day, I was exhausted, out of it and increasingly aware that things were getting dangerous. There was panic, people, instruments and procedures that weren't working. It was, it seemed, too late for a caesarean, but he was badly stuck. Someone got ratty, I wasn't pushing hard enough. Through the gas haze I had this awful moment of clarity: my baby was going to die and it would be my fault.

I'm not entirely sure at what point in the proceedings these thoughts occurred. Before the ventouse? After the arrival of the new doctor? But it stands like an obelisk in that whole gas-blasted memory. Was it the thing that made me push extra hard? Or was it the thing that flicked a different and unwelcome switch?

I know the clock on the wall to my right was a focal point but each time I looked at it I was surprised at how oddly unpredictable the passage of time could be. Finally, not in terms of clock time, but in terms of life time, essence of time, his head got yanked out and a female voice announced with some surprise "Oh, he's looking up at the world." This apparently explained the delay. The rest of him followed and he was whisked off for a once-over by a lady in green. She was pregnant and I felt sure she must have been having second thoughts. Another lady in green was working on me, practising her needlepoint. They stopped fighting me over the gas.

The child, my child was alive. Allegedly so was I. The people in green seemed happy, relieved that he was well. I know people whose parental pride begins with Apgar scores. I wasn't that tuned in; I was just glad he was well. In the antenatal classes (special well-intentioned but intrinsically sad ones for single girls) they'd told us that following the birth some women were not overwhelmed with love or an urge to bond. It wasn't that they didn't love their babies, it was just that they wanted a break, to have a rest, pull themselves together, get stuck into the fig rolls.

At that time I would have been six or seven months pregnant, feeling well, not yet too uncomfortable or ungainly, full of that permanent cuddle and him and me against the world rush of unfamiliarly profound love. I thought that a woman who preferred fig rolls to bonding must surely be heartless.

The needlepoint was ongoing so I was still lying flat when my son was finally handed to me, when we had that first face-to-face meeting for which I had so longed. He was presented to me wrapped in a green blanket, his face and head bleeding, his skull the most peculiar cone shape. He looked so angry. Although granted, I had inhaled about 90 litres of Entonox, so my judgement might have been a little off. I wanted to see him, I wanted to hold him, I wanted to know he was okay. But I was shocked to realise that what I really wanted, what I was overwhelmed with, was a need to recover. I wanted to drink that milky tea and eat those fig rolls, two things I hate. I desperately wanted to sleep. And I felt instantly bad that I must surely be heartless.

For all the hard work that went into the needlepoint, the area never quite recovered. My belly has never been the same again and breasts don't regain their former glory either. But by far the greatest damage was that moment of thinking I was inadequate, unworthy, feeling the wrong thing, heartless. I may never know whether it was a disconnect that happened in the instant when I thought he was going to die, or more precisely that my failure was going to kill him, or some kind of post-traumatic stress response to the pain and fear, or whether it was simply the way I was or am. This was my first shot at childbirth; I didn't know it wasn't always like that so I didn't know I wasn't coping especially badly. I certainly felt overwhelmed and inadequate, I certainly felt robbed of the childbirth and feelings I had imagined, but whatever it was, I knew that other people have much worse things happen and cope much better. Whatever the reason, the bond I had felt from the moment I knew I was carrying that baby (he might have been a girl for a while, but he was never a zygote or an embryo or a foetus, always a baby) did not feel so strong when he was born. And for many years I couldn't find it in my heart to forgive myself for that.

At about 9.00 a.m., we'd been wheeled to the semi-private room my VHI covered and had fallen instantly asleep, although even in my haze it felt weird to have my child outside me. How was I supposed to protect him if I was asleep? By 11.30 a.m. we were awake again. I was so not ready to wake up but my poor child was howling; there was blood on his cot sheet – his head had been cut by implements at the crown and on the temple – and he was howling and scowling. They'd put a plaster on the crown that looked like a bow, he had wispy black hair, and the beginnings of jaundice. He looked like a tiny Mafioso, dressed in one of the white velour babygros I'd shopped for in M&S.

I may have been superstitious and refused to count my chickens, but shopping for the baby who has dislodged your internal organs is one of the great pleasures. They'd said he would be big and as we gazed in awe upon the soon-to-be-filled tiny newborn vests and babygros, my mother and I wondered if this upcoming bruiser mightn't be too big for them. They weren't wrong; he was 9lb 1oz, 57cm long, but the babygro was hanging off him. Newborns are always so much scrawnier than you think. Those little saggy-skinned bums and thighs actually take months to get the clichéd baby-pudgy.

The Mafioso's mother had the biggest gas hangover in the history of the world and the epidural had worn off. This meant that I felt highly nauseous and that while most of me felt uncomfortable, there were two counterpoints of agony that throbbed intermittently: head, general lower torso area, head, general lower torso area . . .

They encouraged me to shower. I was reluctant to be conscious, much less active. Funny how your boundaries slip; twelve hours before I'd been booting spectators out of rooms when they'd been checking my blood pressure, yet here I was showering in all my leaky post birth glory with a strange woman in the room – the nurse, in case I fell down. Oh I really didn't feel too good. Everything had to

be checked, everything. Did I know my bladder was full?
Nope. I got a catheter. Because I was planning on breastfeeding
they couldn't give me anything stronger than Panadol by
way of pain relief, although they could, to protect the
needlepoint, administer a medicine to stop me having a
"bowel motion" for ten days. You have to know me to know
how earthy-crunchy "it's only nature" I am NOT. Could
the students come in and have a look? No.

My poor cranky baby was given Calpol because they
thought his head must be agony. We gave the feeding a shot;
lo and behold, there was nothing natural about that either.
He was too sore to latch on properly, but latching on
improperly is both painful and unproductive. "Can I just
hold your nipple there now, Mum?" I have rarely felt so
bovine. Which you mightn't mind if the child was actually
getting fed.

About lunchtime the visitors started coming in –
grandparents first, that's an emotional one. Then, especially
on a first baby, the oddest mix of visitors, friends, relatives,
work colleagues, from close to distant, most of whom don't
know each other. Neither child nor I felt so good, and there
we were hosting a cocktail party.

"He's gorgeous!" "How are you feeling?" "How was
it?" "Will you ever have sex again?" You mumble your
thanks and say you're fine, it seems churlish to accept the
bunch of roses and say your bum is killing you and that
there's no need to lie, you can see the child looks like an
alien. "What's that?" The curious ask about the bag of
liquid dangling from beneath the bed covers. "Oh. Right."

What I need, desperately need, is sleep. A good run of it.
But I can't. I'm afraid someone will steal my baby if I close

my eyes. I'm still not used to him being out there and he's not big into sleeping long stretches. Also, they wake me to take my blood pressure and the 17-year-old in the next bed who seems to be coping infinitely better than me has at least 75 people around her bed from 10.00 a.m. to midnight, half of whom giggle at the merest hint of a bosom being brandished albeit for the purposes of feeding a baby.

I do like holding him, looking at him, examining all those tiny little pieces of him. I learn to bathe him, to tend his umbilical cord, to dress him, to feed him. I'm so afraid he'll break. But I feel like I'm really not up to the task. I feel sick and sore and scared and tired and utterly overwhelmed. I feel so bad that my physical discomforts outweigh my maternal joy. I feel sorry for this baby getting me as a mother. And I am convinced that he hates me. That sounds nuts, I know that sounds nuts, I knew then it sounded nuts, so nuts I couldn't say it to anyone, but I was convinced he hated me and that this was no less than I deserved.

They said that if I could afford to stay in hospital longer I should. I didn't need to be asked twice. I was terrified of taking over my motherhood. I had my parents and great friends and support. I was not alone, but I felt alone. Mostly because I could never tell anyone how I felt. For months I became increasingly convinced that he hated me, that I was bad for him and that he would die. I went back to work too soon, not through choice, I took on too much and didn't ask for enough help. I never took the time to recover properly, to deal with what was wrong, to learn to cope. I looked after him obsessively but didn't properly bond. I was clearly depressed. And I don't think I stopped being depressed for years.

At least part of it is down to sensing that I wasn't feeling what I was supposed to feel. You're allowed to feel tired, you're just about allowed to let your personal appearance slip for a week or two. But you're not allowed to feel anything less than ecstasy.

And that's dangerous. I can't have been the only one out there, the only new mother who felt overwhelmed and inadequate. So many of us are used to feeling in control of our lives, yet suddenly, those controlled lives are at the mercy of a tiny creature. The guilt, the shame, the pain, the sadness, they're not easy anyway; but you're half-bonkers after you have a baby. Throw those into the mix and it's like trying to climb out of a well.

So, for anyone who feels, has felt or will feel like that, you're not alone and there's nothing intrinsically wrong with you. Whether it takes time, sleep or professional help, it does get better. And maybe it's all the sweeter for those ignominious beginnings.

We've come a long way, that baby and I. He's a tall, daily taller, kind, handsome, funny, clever, cheeky, loud, forgetful, maddening, loving, open soul. And I'm biased. Because I'm his mother. And I love him in a way I never knew was possible.

Áine O'Connor writes the "Smug Married" column in the Sunday Independent. *She is married, lives in Dublin and has two children (the second of whom was substantially easier to achieve).*

Unconditional Love:
A Two-way Street

Liz O'Donnell

Children are a blessing; part of the bounty of life and dogged proof of our humanity. Some children by accident of birth are dealt a difficult hand in the game of life. Others are privileged to know only love and protection and the best of the material world. I have seen children born in African poverty destined to die of preventable disease. Perfect babies in every way save where they were born. The grief of an African mother when her child dies of hunger or disease is just as great as the death of a prince to a king.

For all of us the birth of a child is a life-altering experience. In the western world the birth experience is generally an occasion of celebration and wonder. Our grandparents, lacking the benefit of medical science and contraception, would often have experienced infant deaths. Child mortality rates have greatly improved in our developed world and these days in Ireland the birth of children is a highly medical affair with excellent outcomes for mother and baby. New mothers can be home within three days of giving birth. Personally, I disagree with this "roll-on, roll-off" process and would like to see a return to the week-long stay in a hospital or nursing home for young mothers.

The euphoria, or "over the moon" feeling is common to all new parents but too often there is an unhelpful conspiracy of silence about the physical realities and trauma of the birth experience for many women.

The compelling recollection of the birth of my first child is a feeling of having been totally misled by all the books, classes and conversations about childbirth. So this offering may serve to forewarn young mothers of information denied to them.

I was young, healthy, well rested, and ready for the great event. The day came and went. Two weeks passed, pacing up and down Pigeon House pier in voluminous frocks billowing in the summer breeze and I considered everything from cod liver oil to vodka to bring it on. My doctor was calm to the point of slumber about my plight. I was demented, afraid that my child was dead in my womb. I had no movements (there being no room I expect) but each examination was uneventful. "When the apple is ready to fall, it will just happen," said my mother, but I feared the worst.

Eventually, after much pleading, I was to be induced. There followed the breaking of waters and drip-induced contractions and what was to become a totally unnatural and painful birth of a beautiful girl twelve hours later. I genuinely fell in love with my midwife. My poor husband was appalled to witness such intensity of suffering. In retrospect, guys should have a choice on attendance rather than be steamrolled by modernity.

My own mother and father were first in, having been waiting in the wings. As I gazed at my baby in my mother's arms, I wept with joy, but longed for her to take over now. I was so tired, sore and shocked at the birth experience, I felt totally incapable of minding this child.

It was a time before mobile phones, so calls meant a painful trip and queue for the pay phone in the dreary hospital corridor. If all this sounds maudlin, it was. My baby was perfect, beautiful and healthy, and I was miserable. No amount of talk about the "baby blues" could shake me out of it. I needed to be minded.

Which is where my mother Carmel came in. She moved into our house for six weeks and nursed me back to health when I came out of hospital. When I did a feed, which was on demand, she would whisk the baby off in the pram down Sandymount Strand, proclaiming that babies need air, food and routine, nothing else.

Slowly my energy and spirit returned. But it was almost a reversion to childhood for me, at the same time as I was being transformed into a mother myself. This was the big truth which emerged from the birth of my first child. I appreciated for the first time the unconditional love of a mother for her child; a bond gliding through the generations like an umbilical cord. I was forever linked to my mother and grandmother and now to my daughter.

The arrival of my second child was a very different experience. From the start it was more difficult. Looking after a toddler and being heavily pregnant meant there were no lazy days just resting and reading baby books as before.

Again, the "happy gang" came to the rescue – my mother Carmel and her two older sisters Anna and Mona. They would arrive clattering down Seafort Avenue to our little cottage, laden down with scones, jam, hand knits and three pairs of hands to do whatever needed to be done.

The baby was breach and a section was recommended. After my first experience, I was delighted at the prospect of any alternative. But that too was to be denied. By some miracle of manipulation that doesn't bear thinking about, Mr Darling turned the baby in utero. Yes, I kid you not. I was heading for the same tunnel of pain as before.

The love affair began. From the beginning, this boy broke my heart; I could not feed him. The instinct to nurture is animal. It consumed me as he did over those first weeks of breastfeeding. The nightmare of colic appeared. The struggle to feed was agonising to baby and all concerned. Gripewater being dribbled into his gaping mouth is a lasting memory. I fled to the local doctor in panic; he recommended earplugs and patience. My mother, wise as always, declared that there were no medals for breastfeeding and produced a bottle. The colic continued but at least I could be helped by others and my body was returned to me.

The sibling rivalry started early. My toddler daughter fired occasional missiles into the baby crib with mixed success. Two babies in nappies is a life of stooping. My back was broken from bending down to do everything from changing nappies to bathing to picking up Lego. The long seafront walks, which were so much part of my life with Laura, were now rendered impossible when faced with the blank refusal of a toddler to walk. Like many parents I resorted to the video as a salvation.

Looking back, it seems incredible, but I had no help! Because I had given up work I felt I had to do it all myself. I began to identify with sleep deprivation as a method of torture. I could hardly believe that this was the confident woman who had run a busy legal office and enjoyed a social whirl.

Overall, there was a tendency towards self-pity and isolation. All around me friends and colleagues were advancing their brilliant legal careers. I was the only one of our group to be home alone with two babies and crashing confidence. Yet it had been my decision to give up work to care for the children full-time.

Sure, there were blissful times of intimacy and wonder with the children. They became my whole life's focus. Unreasonable fears also appeared. Fear that an awful disease would take one or both of them away; that my husband would be killed on treacherous roads in mid-winter; that some awful catastrophe would happen in the world, like a nuclear explosion, to devastate the futures of my children. I could barely watch the news, such was my anxiety at the doom-laden diet being broadcast. Famines and wars freaked me out. All violent movies were out of the question. My brain had gone to mush. Reading was impossible with two small children.

We moved house to a lovely quiet road in Rathmines and we had lovely neighbours with small children. Most of the mothers, however, were still working full-time, so my daytime isolation persisted. Radio was my lifeline from early morning and BBC 4 provided intellectual stimulation. Laura was now at playschool in the mornings, so I had the freedom to enjoy the baby as he toddled around. He was a wonderful toddler, curious and contented. Things were looking up as my brain started to function again with full nights' sleep.

One morning as I gazed lovingly into his blue eyes laced with blond lashes, I noticed he went into a little trance and his eyelids fluttered – almost vibrated – for about forty seconds. I was mystified, as this had not happened before. I continued to monitor him for the remainder of the morning and the episodes recurred at regular intervals, occasionally accompanied by a tremor in his arm. During these brief absences or interruptions he was not distressed, just absent. Soon after, we were in Our Lady's Hospital for Sick Children in Crumlin, with my beautiful boy wired up to an EEG machine. Mild epilepsy was the verdict. Suddenly all my hopes and dreams for this beautiful boy were dashed. What did it mean for his future life?

Epilum, an anticonvulsant, was to be taken several times a day. I was devastated. This was a permanent disability with unclear outcomes. Would these absences develop into full-blown fits? I felt as if something precious had been taken away from us, our perfect child. High temperatures were danger zones. Flickering lights had to be avoided as they could bring on an episode.

There was never a child more watched, monitored or observed. I read up all the books on epilepsy but brain waves in children or any brain injury can be part of such a broad spectrum. Each brain is unique and the illness is different in each child. Thankfully although on medication until he was eleven years old, it seems he grew out of it in adolescence.

In life, perhaps the hardest and most challenging job is that of being a parent. There is no training for this immense task of caring for and nurturing one's offspring to maturity. For me, having children was the beginning of responsibility in the true sense of the word. Before, I had lived a life which had no limitations. Once a parent, one is responsible legally, emotionally and physically for others.

We tend to parent as we have been parented. In my case, I had been blessed with a blissfully happy and properly functioning family. Both of my parents were emotionally and physically present to their children. My mother was a full-time mother who only occasionally worked outside the home. I grew up surrounded by her sisters and my grandmother in a closely knit extended family. My father, a Guinness worker, was a constant presence in our lives because he worked shifts and was always there when we came home from school to take us to the beach or the park for walks. They rarely went out in the evenings as a couple. Their whole lives were devoted to us. They put no pressure on us as children. Our best was always enough. We were fortunate as a family to have the security of a paternalistic employer in Guinness. It was said that to be a Guinness worker was akin to being the aristocracy of the working class. It was true. We never had luxuries but we always had plenty compared to our neighbours in the north inner city of Dublin where we lived in the harsh 1950s.

So, the challenge for me as a parent in the 1980s was to come as close as possible to achieving that model which had served me so well as a child. The world was so different, so much more sophisticated. That we had more money to spend didn't really help. Time was what we had less of, given the demanding careers we had chosen. I was fortunate to have the support of extended family in the rearing of my children. I can honestly say that my parents were a huge part of my children's development for which I will be forever grateful.

Many couples are not so lucky and experience huge strain trying to raise small children without any external support. The nuclear family is a tight fit, with very little room for flexibility. Children seeking attention to which they are entitled can find themselves in a constant battle with distressed and overworked parents. My advice to young working parents is to put in place structured and constant contact with grandparents and wider family members. Build up a network of support and liaison and a web of other adults to whom your children can relate. This can take a bit of effort but will reap real results in terms of diversity of activity and influence for your children. Nuclear families can be stifling both for parents and children. We all need space and room to have different relationships with people wider than the immediate family.

Another aspect of being a parent is that it can awaken a much more heightened awareness of politics, not only domestically but globally. Very close to the birth of my first child, Laura, the terrible calamity of the Chernobyl explosion occurred. My sense of outrage and shock at such a global disaster was intensified by the fact that my little child was potentially at risk. I became much more aware of environmental matters and world peace. I wanted my child to live a life without the experience of war and calamity as I had. Suddenly, there was talk of toxic clouds carrying radiation from Belarus as far as Scotland, affecting sheep and poisoning the atmosphere. With Sellafield just across the water, the spectre of a similar incident was no longer just a fantasy.

I began to notice the dearth of women in public life. I noted how women pushing buggies were made to feel a nuisance in shops and public transport. I noted how people treat you differently when you have two children hanging out of you in the bank. I noticed a reduction in status, rather than an elevation. I noticed inequality. In retrospect, I now see that becoming a parent politicised me.

Perhaps the most frequent question asked of me during my life in politics over fifteen years was how I managed to balance family and work. My answer has always been "with difficulty". Most working parents struggle in this regard and for women who work outside the home, there is constant guilt about short-changing the children because of their work or career. Politics, however, is perhaps uniquely difficult in this regard.

Firstly, it is tailor-made for men who are either single or have supportive wives who do not work outside the home. Most political activity takes place in the evenings. The Dáil, for example, sits until 8.30 and often later, so one is not home until at least eleven when the children and frequently the exhausted spouse are asleep. Depending on the constituency, weekends can be ring-fenced for family, when not a minister, but I had a five-year ministerial stint, which was awesomely demanding in terms of time and preoccupation.

Most kids just want regular parents as a backdrop to their lives. I remember my young son begging me not to put on my "meeting face" as I applied lipstick to go to work. They can be teased at school about their unusual parent. They may feel short-changed and they are right. What to do? Personally, I found myself in a job which stimulated me and which gave me many opportunities to use my talents in public service. We only have one life to live and choices have to be made in balancing life's responsibilities. This dilemma is not unique to politicians. All demanding and responsible careers carry levels of stress and preoccupation which naturally conflict with the demands of children for attention.

My children are now young adults. In time, hopefully they will reflect and not judge their mother for long absences and choices made. Having them and rearing them to the best of my ability has been the most challenging task of my life. And just as my beloved parents still worry about me, I shall continue to fret over my offspring as they navigate their own lives as adults. Ultimately, one hopes it is a matter of unconditional love which goes both ways.

Liz O'Donnell is a former Government Minister and Progressive Democrats TD. She represented Dublin South from 1992 to 2007 and was Minister of State at the Department of Foreign Affairs from 1997 to 2002. She now works in media and public affairs consultancy.

The Rocky Road to Motherhood

Mary O'Rourke

I suppose if I am going to write about my family I'd better go back to the very beginning. I myself was the youngest in a family of four. I had what I think looking back was a happy, involved childhood. But I had no inbuilt ideas of what I would want myself if and when I got married, what size of a family, etc.

But I knew early on that I did want to get married and that I wanted babies, and lots of them.

Fast forward to when I was 18 and met Enda O'Rourke, who proved to be the love of my life. We engaged in a very strong boyfriend/girlfriend relationship which culminated in our marriage on 14 September 1960. I was 22 and he was 24.

I was mad wild about Enda – loved his looks and was overcome by love and, if I am honest, lust as well. In my day you didn't go to bed with your guy until you had tied the marriage knot. Perhaps it sounds quaint now but that was the way it was. Of course, we lived in holy terror all the time, often skating very near the edge but determined that we wouldn't fall into sin, so to speak. Nevertheless, we were engaging in lustful activities but staying just this side of what was right/wrong.

Anyway, back to our wedding day. Away we went and, of course, I thought children would come pretty instantly. My two brothers and my sister, much older than me, had all got married in the one year and each of them had produced child numbers one, two and three in quick succession. So I thought this would be my fate also.

But it was not to be. It was the first real lesson I got in life: no matter how much in love you are with your husband, and he with you, and no matter how much you want to become pregnant and to be a mother sometimes it just does not happen. What you really really want you might not always get.

Year one went by and then year two and year three, with no sign of conception from me – and it certainly was not lack of trying on our part. We were very deeply in love and could not get our heads around why it was just not happening for us. Everywhere we looked, both within our family and outside among our friends, all the females were supporting ever-growing bumps which soon transformed into a lovely baby and it seemed happiness all around. It was not happening for us.

In a way this setback brought us even closer together. I was very determined that I was going to have a baby, so when year three had passed I went to Dublin to meet with a very eminent gynaecologist Dr Éamon de Valera. (I can hear the readers saying, "Oh, she would go to him." Be that as it may, he was one of the country's foremost gynaecologists.) During his cursory examination, he said, "You seem a fine healthy young woman, but of course I would have to meet Enda."

Now I am talking about a time over 40 years ago, when nobody ever wrote or spoke about fertility or dwelt upon the issue, least of all the guy in the household. Anyway, home I went on the train and I told Enda what the doctor had said. Enda said, "Why not? Of course I will go and see him." So the appointment was made and Dr de Valera examined us both in the Mater and announced that Enda and I were fit and well. I will always hold in my mind the letter Enda got some days later from Dr de Valera's office saying that his sperm was 100 per cent mobile. Enda let out a wild yippee.

So there we were, full of life and full of hope. Six months later I conceived. To this day I am convinced that it happened because I was in the throes of a very bad flu and confined to bed. The dates show up that it was during this period that I conceived.

I loved the idea of being pregnant and I loved the idea of my bump getting bigger and I loved the idea of swanning around all my friends saying, "We did it." I felt a bit like Barack Obama must have felt – "Yes, we can. Yes, we can" – and yes, we did.

In due course, on 3 August 1964, our son Feargal Patrick Thomas O'Rourke was born, 7½ pounds, a model baby with a big head of dark hair. We adored him.

So home I came with my prize booty and we were now a real married couple with our baby boy but of course as in all things in life, another difficulty arose. Feargal was colicky and cried a lot and I developed postnatal depression, a right dose of it. Edna would often come home and find me with Feargal on my knee tears falling from my eyes and Feargal yelling his lungs out. I got good medical help and I rapidly recovered, never again to be plagued by nerves of any kind throughout my life, thank God.

We loved Feargal dearly and deeply. I remember when we would put him down at night Enda would stand by the little cot and say imagine, "Mary, you and I made him." The creation of a child is the most wonderful activity. When one thinks of the complexity of arriving at it, you wonder again at God's wishes for us and it has often made me think of the whole issue of creativity. Now I was as good as my brothers Brian and Paddy and my sister Anne, who were festooned with children, and both Enda and I had proven our worth in producing a wonderful baby boy.

Time went on and, of course, I thought that, having unleashed the forces of fecundity, I had nothing to do but wait until I conceived child number two, but this was not to be. Again year one, year two, year three passed; again, even with our intense love for one another and our intense enjoyment of conjugal activity, I did not conceive. Why? Why? Why?

So it was back to Dr de Valera again. Wily old bird, he certainly knew more about my health than he ever admitted. Having done his examination and told me I was still healthy, quite out of the blue he asked me, "Have you and Enda thought of adoption?" We had discussed it endlessly together at home in between trying to pinpoint our correct times in the ovulation cycle for conception. We were both very keen on the idea.

So we embarked on that and when I went to see Dr de Valera again I said to him, yes, that we would both be happy about that and he said he would arrange it.

So on 4 September 1968, I received a telephone call from Dr de Valera to say that Enda and I had a beautiful new son. We went to Dublin together with Feargal and we met our lovely new baby, six days old and absolutely beautiful with dark hair and pale skin. I immediately felt a surge of physical love for him. I know this sounds fanciful, but I really felt this child had come out of me, even though I knew it did not happen. I felt the same flood of love and Enda felt the same. I have always rationalised it in this way: that Feargal came out of me but Aengus came into my heart.

We christened him Aengus John O'Rourke and he was a delight as a baby, quiet and placid but showing early signs of liveliness, smiling early. Every year on 4 September, Aengus's birthday, I think about his birth mother. I would love her to know that Aengus is such a joy and brought such great happiness to us as a family. Reflecting on adoption, in this day and age it is quite a regular thing for people to do, but it is overseas adoption. In our time, it was much rarer.

Aengus and Feargal, aged four, quickly established a rapport, though of course there was the odd dash of jealousy. Feargal was a bit bemused about it all and I am sure as he grew up and found out the facts of life he learned very quickly that you just did not go to Dublin and get a baby like that. Feargal had been the centre of life *chez* O'Rourke, and now he had to share the limelight with this baby Aengus but by and large they struck up a relationship which is strong and robust to this day.

We had been very mobile with one child but we quickly found that two children is another kettle of fish, so to speak, and the preparation for moving, shifting, visiting and travelling was twice as burdensome but always a joy. We were now a packet of a family – mom, dad and two little boys. What more could one want in life? I was so happy with life.

I never fell pregnant again, despite continuing in a very good physical harmonious life with Enda. I always felt that one child in a family, blessed although it is, sometimes appears to be a lonely figure.

Of course, parenthood brings joys but also massive challenges. Everyone wants the best for their children – after all, everyone's duck is a swan – but I feel that some of the real joys for Enda and I were watching two boys growing up together, helping one another. Feargal always took on the role of elder brother in a very serious fashion – looking out for Aengus in the playground in national school, etc.

Actually their views on going to primary school were so markedly different. Feargal roared crying every day – and on reflection, I should not have let him go at four as he really wasn't ready for it – whereas Aengus took to it like a duck to water. With the help of his little pal Gilly, he trotted off every day full of hope and full of expectation that school was going to be great, and it was for him.

The boys went to the local Marist primary school and then the local Marist secondary school. Aengus went through a wild phase in his late teens and, like all parents, we worried endlessly about him. But he never stopped confiding in me as his mother. On a Sunday night I would often be ironing for the week ahead and he would come beside me into the kitchen and strike up a conversation and away we would go. We often ironed out many growing difficulties like that. I learned a fair lesson from that: never stop communication and always seek to open up avenues so that even if there is tension in a relationship, it can be worked through.

Skipping years, Feargal and Aengus later married, Feargal living in Dublin with two children and Aengus living in Athlone with three children.

My darling Enda passed away and it took me a long long while to come to grips with life after that, but the coming of the grandchildren greatly eased the sorrow and each new bright birth heralded renewed hope again. Children and grandchildren make up the skein of life and I am so grateful for my lovely sons, my daughters-in-law and truly lovely grandchildren.

So every weekend in Athlone my days are made lively by Luke, Sarah and James, who are Aengus's and Lisa's three children, and from time to time in Dublin and or in Athlone, Feargal and Maeve's two children, Jennifer and Sam, come to stay.

People have always told me that grandchildren are wonderful, and they are because somehow it is as if you have a chance again to deal with your children and you see them mirrored in the bright shining faces around you. Life is now ahead for them and I am so happy to be part of their extended lives.

I hope all these children grow up with the love of life and of family and I hope they have bright optimistic natures. To my mind, to have an optimistic spirit is one of the greatest gifts you can have. Whenever I feel really down, a good sleep enables me to hop up the next morning ready for whatever life throws at me again. I often think of the words of Shakespeare: *"sleep that knits up the ravelled sleeve of care"*.

Mary O'Rourke is a Fianna Fáil TD, serving in the Longford-Westmeath constituency, and a former Government Minister.

Free at Last

John Waters

I'm not sure that it is correct to say that having children changes you. This is an approximate way of seeing it, because certainly you end up different to the way you were before. Indeed, it would be strange if you did not. But the idea of "change" suggests something arbitrary, a random process that takes hold of one's present condition and moulds it into another, much as though, having lived in the same place for several decades, you have taken off to some exotic place.

But the "change" that happens on becoming a parent is like the change of the sapling into the tree, or the caterpillar into the butterfly: it is not arbitrary, it is not a form of renovation, it is not random. It is really a discovering of your essential nature, after a time of growth in curiosity and experiment. It is a coming home rather than a journey to a new place. It is natural, not merely in its effects but in that it is, or should be, predictable. To the extent that it is not predictable, this unpredictability is a function of our flawed culture, which has a dwindling sense of the meaning of parenthood, and in particular of fatherhood.

For me, becoming a parent brought many things which I did not anticipate. It woke me up to myself and to my true nature and structure. It returned me to a sense of my dependence, my mortality, my desire. It changed my sense of what freedom was. It pulled me back to the now, jerking me out of the future as though I had been lassoed. It opened my eyes to the specific: to the sense that, at a certain key moment, one must choose one road rather than another, now, or at least after a little thought, and that these decisions are much less vital for their outcomes than for their nowness.

One quality with which my daughter Róisín put me in touch was the necessity for particularity. Having been born of the Peter Pan generations that emerged from the revolutionary 1960s, I had acquired a way of looking at the world that to me seemed natural but is actually anything but. It was evasive, fragmented, contradictory, confused. Having revolted against authority and truth, our generations had come to believe that we could muddle through life without seeming to take strong lines on anything. We would not be dogmatic, didactic or entrenched on our perspectives. We would be open, tolerant, pluralistic. Everything was relative, after all, and who could say where the truth lay?

But this does not work with children. With a child you cannot postpone the necessity for clarity. It is not so much that you have to have an answer, right now, even if it's the wrong one, though you certainly do need to have lots of answers and it is better if a majority of them turn out to be right. But, more than that, being a parent demands that you have reached a conclusion. It requires particularity, specificity. Everything is not relative. Some things are good and others bad, and likewise with people. Tolerance is fine, but sometimes it invites danger. Thinking purely for yourself, it is possible to get by without making definite decisions about what you believe, what you stand for, where you are going, but having a child means that you have to start thinking through all the things you spent several decades avoiding coming to conclusions about.

Thus, there is this paradox, whereby as a parent you are supposed to be teaching your child in preparation for the life she is to live, in truth she ends up teaching you about the life you have already lived. Being a father was for me an awakening to life, to the world and, most of all, to myself. It was in this role, after 40 years of puzzlement and confusion, that I began to see myself for what I was, and the process of life for what it is. It brought me back to fundamentals. It was, therefore, in the purest sense possible, a religious experience.

I have written before about the moment when my daughter Róisín was just a few weeks old and she came to me, for the first time, to stay overnight at my house. I had been with her through a good few nights before that, but always with other people around. It was, of course, a strange sensation, to wake in the night and hear the breathing in the cot beside my bed, and then be struck by the realisation that this was . . . my child! I could not wait to take her home with me. But then a strange moment arrived, when I put her to bed for the first time in what would become our home together, read her a story and watched her fall asleep. Then, as I went to leave the room, I stopped at the door to look back at her sleeping countenance. And then I realised that I found myself unable to leave. The idea that I, for the first time, had sole responsibility for this delicate creature filled me with dread. I stopped in the doorway and watched her. I left the room for a few moments and listened to her breathing on the baby monitor in the living room. Then I returned to the room and stood watching her again. What was I going to do? How could I sleep this night and leave her alone? Who would watch over her, protect her? I spent an hour or two wrestling with this dilemma before it began to dawn on me that it was not I who kept my daughter alive, any more than it was I who kept myself alive. Her life was dependent on something far greater than either of us, and this would sustain her whether I was there or not.

It transported me back to a certain moment in my childhood when, following the sudden death of the father of a friend of mine, I developed an obsessive fear that my own father, too, would die suddenly in his sleep. Perhaps that moment was the beginning or something, or the first concrete evidence of something that had long since begun: a loss of faith, certainly, but something else also – the development of a false understanding of reality and of my own structure.

When, in a fundraising effort on behalf of the Irish Hospice Foundation, I conceived the Millennium fund-raising project that would become known as *The Whoseday Book*, in which 366 writers and artists were invited to submit a short piece for a particular day, I chose 10 March, my daughter's birthday, and wrote what was really my first and only poem about this moment, "Raidio Róisín":

> "I called it Raidio Róisín, the baby monitor I used to place near your cot while you slept. It reminded me of your grandfather, who died seven years before you arrived. I wished I had had one back then, to check on him in the night, to ascertain whether he was still breathing, rather than crouching at the bedroom door with my ear to the keyhole, listening for sounds of life. I wished I had had one on the morning he died, so I could have reached his side to say goodbye. Once, while living in our apartment in Colville Terrace, Londing Town, I discovered that there was another baby on the other channel, to whose breathing I had been listening for an hour by mistake. But the first sign was a bum note that sent me scrambling for the tuner. For a moment I fretted that you might have been awake and calling me. But the moment passed, for in truth I did not need the monitor. Always I would wake two minutes before you stirred, and lie there waiting. There was a time in my life when this might have seemed a massive inconvenience. But, whenever it happened, I'd find myself longing for your cry, so I could see your face again."

So, one of the first things being a father did for me was return me to a position of trust – trust in something I did not understand, but of which the experience of living had provided me with a sense, because now I had no choice. At this moment, I think, there was a reintegration of my reason, which in my adulthood had become waylaid by the prevailing cultural ideas that reason has to do exclusively with demonstrability. But, really, what passes for reason in our societies is merely scepticism born of a deep pessimism, itself born of fear. Perhaps from that moment when I heard the news that my friend's father had died, I had been unable to trust. But now, with a fragile child in the house, I had only one choice: trust or go crazy.

The final lines of that prose-poem convey also something else my daughter unexpectedly gave me. The idea that waiting for her to wake so I could get out of bed on a cold morning and spend an hour feeding her and talking to her, to my pre-existing self would have seemed like an imposition. But it was truly a wonderful experience to be sitting with her at four in the morning as she bounced laughing in her jumpsuit, in a city I was in for no other purpose but to be with her.

In this way, she began to teach me the true meaning of freedom. Most of my life I had accepted the prevailing idea of freedom as relating to the capacity to do as you pleased, to be liberated from responsibility and "free" to enjoy yourself. Unconsciously, in my life, I had long since been dividing my time into "unfree" and "free" time, the former being a price to be paid for the enjoyment of the latter. And yet, when I sat back and looked carefully at this division, I had to admit that the "free" time I so much looked forward to when I was engaged in my "unfreedom" never turned out anything like the promise it held forth in advance.

I became acutely aware of this syndrome in relation to caring for Róisín. Because of the huge responsibility involved, I found myself initially dreading the idea of having to spend several days taking care of my daughter. And for a while, too, while I was doing so, I would find myself longing for the freedom of the following weekend, when I would be footloose and fancy-free.

But it never worked out like this. Usually, when the Friday of my "freedom" would arrive, I would find myself bereft, unable to think of anything I wanted to do, now my baby was not here. I would spend the weekends of my projected freedom wishing her back. And when I looked back over an extended period embracing such "free" and "unfree" periods, I gradually began to see that the moments of greatest enjoyment, and thus of freedom, occurred while I was looking after my child. Freedom was actually the direct opposite of what I had imagined it to be.

Something else my daughter brought me was the capacity to live in the present. Before she came along, I had spent 40 years living in a culture which somehow persuaded me always to be projecting forward, to be hoping for things, expecting things, anticipating things, good and bad. I could live in the past or in the future, often more than 20 or 30 years in either direction, but never in the now. This is the modern condition, the vacuous restlessness inculcated by advertising and market dynamics having opened a void within our souls which we try to fill with distractions, drugs of various kinds. When and where we are now is inadequate and ordinary – every other place or time or company is steeped in a seductive exoticism. Life is elsewhere.

A baby, I soon discovered, is the most powerful antidote to this condition, because a baby leaves you with no choice but to be where you are with it. Once I rumbled the idea of freedom, I began to concentrate on the idea that I was free while I was taking care of my daughter, and this enabled me to enjoy the moment far more than I would have in the absence of this insight.

And this taught me that love is a condition that transcends sentiment. In the course of observing my own responses to the development of the father–child relationship with my daughter, it has occurred to me more than once that, without the more prosaic quantities of duty and responsibility, the pearl I now recognise as love might never have been woven. And without a more fundamental need in myself, it is doubtful if these qualities of duty and responsibility could have been unearthed from the mire of selfhood that is the inner reality of us all. That need can best be described as a desire to assert a version of myself with which I could be happy, could stand over, could believe in. It had to do with the idea of destiny, of living a life that corresponded to some deeper idea of myself, with what we call identity, but also with the idea of being perceived as a good and worthy person.

It takes some of us half our lifetimes to discover what the ancients saw clearly: it is far, far better to give than to receive. After decades of seeking in relationships with others the satisfaction of our own needs by the pursuit of these in a direct and unabashed fashion, we may, if we're lucky enough, one day stumble upon the discovery that the outcome, for ourselves, is actually far better when we put the other's needs ahead of our own. In doing this we unearth in ourselves a capacity for feeling that all our previous self-seeking had no more than glimpsed in the distance. And this, far more than the direct and selfish pursuit of personal happiness, is the engine of human existence.

John Waters is an author, playwright and columnist with The Irish Times. *His latest book is* Lapsed Agnostic.

Free postage *
Worldwide

on our web site
www.poolbeg.com

Direct to your home!

If you enjoyed this book why
not visit our website

and get another book delivered straight to
your home or to a friend's home!

www.poolbeg.com

All orders are despatched within 24 hours

* See web site for details